Contents

KU-415-333

Foreword

This guide to the law is not intended to be used as a substitute for proper legal advice from a solicitor. Professionals may use this guide to inform service users about the law that affects them, but should never give advice on the best course of action to be taken.

The law in this guide is correct as at 31st January 2008.

Part One
The Scottish Legal System

1.0 Civil and Criminal Law

1.1 The Court Hierarchy

1.2 Legal Personnel

1.3 A Case in the Courts

Appendix - Checklist for Witnesses

Part One

The Scottish Legal System

1.0   Civil and Criminal Law

The legal system in Scotland essentially comprises two distinct branches - civil law and criminal law. Both these branches have different court structures and different rules of procedure and evidence (how the case may be proved).

A simple explanation of the difference between civil law and criminal law matters, is that criminal law deals with the conviction, sentencing and punishment of a person, by the state, for having carried out a legal wrong whereas civil law deals with all other aspects of law, such as damages for professional negligence; adoption and divorce; sale of goods and unfair dismissal.

Within each branch of law, there are a number of different courts that form a hierarchy. Logically this allows for a dissatisfied person (or party, as they are called) to appeal a decision to a higher court. Not surprisingly relevant decisions

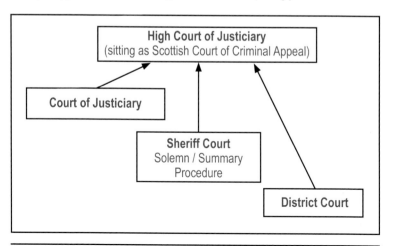

of the higher courts are referred to in the decisions of the lower courts. What is perhaps surprising is that evidence (the means of proving the case such as witnesses or objects) is normally only taken at the initial court (called court of 'first instance') and is not repeated for the appeal court.

1.1 The Court Hierarchy

1.10 Criminal Court Structure

From the above diagram it should be clear that a criminal case might start in the District Court, the Sheriff Court or the High Court of Justiciary. Exactly which court and which procedure will be used depends on the seriousness of the criminal offence. However regardless of where the case is first held, all appeals go to the High Court of Justiciary sitting as the Scottish Court of Criminal Appeal.

1.101 The District Court

This is the lowest court in the criminal hierarchy and it deals with the most basic offences such as breach of the peace, petty theft, minor assault and statutory offences such as non-payment of television licence. Due to the level of offence that can be tried in the District Court, the punishments that can be given are limited. The maximum custodial (prison) sentence that can be imposed by the district court is 60 days imprisonment and the maximum fine is level 4, £2500. The role of judge in the District Court is carried out by a Justice of the Peace (J.P.), who is not legally qualified, although they can be assisted by a legally qualified clerk. In some district courts there may be a panel of J.P., that is more than one. The District Court system is undergoing major changes. Administration of the District Court will move from local authority to the Scottish Court Service and District Courts will be known as JP Courts.

1.102 The Sheriff Court

This is the second lowest court in the hierarchy and deals with more serious cases than those of the District Court. The Sheriff Court operates two different types of criminal procedure and again the difference is due to the seriousness of the offence:

Summary - this is for less serious offences such as minor drug offences, road traffic offences theft and assaults. In the Sheriff Court on summary procedure the sentences that can be imposed are a maximum of 12 months imprisonment or a fine of £10,000. A Sheriff, who is a legally qualified person, performs the role of the judge.

Solemn - this is for more serious offences such as aggravated assault, serious road traffic offences and robbery. Due to the seriousness of these offences the trial is before a Sheriff with a Jury. The jury has the duty to decide whether on the facts and evidence produced the accused person was guilty of the offence. The Sheriff will then decide on the sentence, and may impose a prison sentence of up to five years or an unlimited fine.

1.103   The High Court of Justiciary

This is the highest criminal trial court in Scotland and deals with the most serious cases. Indeed cases involving murder, rape, treason, incest and offences under the Official Secrets Acts may only be tried at the High Court of Justiciary. Technically the court has no permanent home, although in practice it sits almost continually in both Edinburgh and Glasgow. In addition the Court goes on circuit, that is travels around Scotland to major cities, to deal with the most serious of cases. Usually it will hold its hearings in the building of the Sheriff Court. The procedure used in the High Court of Justiciary is solemn procedure, so a judge and a jury hear the case. The judge will be a Lord Commissioner of Justiciary, and as in the solemn cases in the Sheriff court it is the jury who decide on the issue of guilt with the judge deciding on the sentence. The sentencing power of this court is unlimited, although for some cases there is a mandatory sentence, for example for murder the judge must sentence them to life imprisonment.

1.104   Scottish Court of Criminal Appeal

The High Court of Justiciary as the **Scottish Court of Criminal Appeal**

This court hears all criminal appeals in Scotland. Three senior judges of the High Court of Justiciary hear the appeals. Appeals can only be made either against conviction on points of law (not against findings of facts proved) or against sentence.

1.11   Civil Court Structure

From the diagram above it should be clear that most civil cases start in the Sheriff court, albeit that there are three different types of procedure. Some civil cases however start in the Court of Session, Outer House. As with criminal cases, the starting point is determined by the seriousness of the case, which in civil cases tends to be based on the financial value of the matter in dispute.

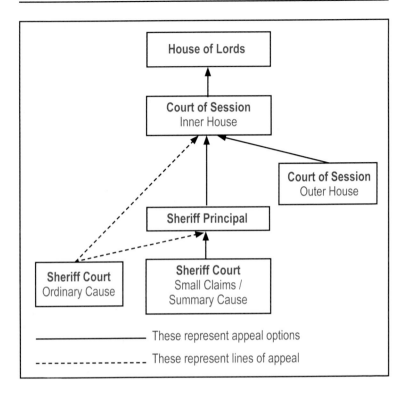

1.110 The Sheriff Court

This is the lowest court in the civil hierarchy, and any dispute for £1500 or less must begin in the Sheriff Court. Essentially the procedure used in the Sheriff Court will depend on the monetary value of the case. Ordinary Cause procedure is used for the higher valued cases and also for family law actions.

1.111 The Sheriff Principal

This is the senior judge in the Sheriffdom/ area. He hears appeals from decisions by Sheriffs within his own sheriffdom/ area.

1.112 The Court of Session

This is divided into two houses:

The Outer House - This is the highest court where a civil case can start. Although based in Edinburgh it hears cases from all over Scotland. The workload is generally the more complicated civil cases, and there are some types of case that must begin there, such as cases for declarator of marriage.

The Inner House - This operates as an appeal court, with normally three judges sitting on each case. Appeals to this court are on points of law only.

1.113   The House of Lords

The House of Lords - Final appeal can be taken to the Judicial Committee of the House of Lords. All are legally qualified, senior judges. A panel of five judges normally hears cases. Very few Scottish cases proceed to appeal to the House of Lords

1.2   Legal Personnel

1.20   Solicitors

Solicitors are the GPs of the legal world. Most firms of solicitors provide a broad range of legal services covering the spectrum from civil law to criminal law, although individual solicitors may tend to specialise on particular areas. The solicitor can provide advice and may appear in the lower courts on behalf of their clients. Unless the solicitor has undertaken additional qualification to become a solicitor advocate, they cannot appear for a client in either the High Court of Justiciary or the Court of Session. In such cases the solicitor will instruct an advocate. In more recent years a number of solicitors have become members of CALM (Comprehensive Accredited Lawyer Mediators). Mainly this service helps to resolve matrimonial disputes through a process of mediation (facilitated discussion between the parties involved) rather than through the court action. The law provides for protection of the confidentiality of the solicitor client relationship by preventing a solicitor being called to court to give evidence of their discussions with their client. This is called the legal professional privilege. It extends to cover discussions with lawyer mediators. Solicitors are members of the Law Society of Scotland. They can be instructed not only by those over 16 but also by children. This is especially important in family matters where by law the child has a right to express their view.

1.21   Advocates

Advocates are the court specialists and generally are involved in representing clients in the higher courts (Court of Session or the High Court of Justiciary) or in giving opinions to solicitors as to the likelihood of success on a particular point of law. These opinions are referred to as Counsel's opinion.Unlike solicitors advocates do not have a High Street presence and are not capable of being instructed except through other professionals such as solicitors.

1.22   Judges: Justices of the Peace; Sheriffs; Lords Ordinary

Although the qualification and powers of a judge vary depending on the court in which they sit, essentially all judges fill the same role. Unless there is a jury, the judge must decide on the facts as established by the evidence led and the legal consequence of these facts, that is do these facts prove that the accused murdered the victim? If there is a jury the judge must give direction to the jury to advise them on what facts must be established to find the person guilty. Thereafter the judge must decide on the appropriate remedy - in criminal cases this will usually be a sentence, whilst in civil cases this could be finding a person entitled to payment, granting a divorce or declaring persons to be married. (see the section on remedies)

1.23   Procurator Fiscal

Legally qualified persons employed as civil servants with the job of investigating, raising and presenting court proceedings for criminal offences. It is the procurator fiscal, not the police, which decides whether a case is to be brought to court.

1.24   Sheriff Clerk

Civil servant who is responsible for administration within the Sheriff court. The sheriff clerk's office is a good place to get advice regarding actions that are going to court.

1.25   Sheriff Officers

Officers of the sheriff court who amongst other duties serve (deliver) court documents and carry out warrant sales.

1.3   A Case in the Courts

1.30   Prior to the Court Hearing

Civil
In civil cases the initial process is through written documents lodged with the court. Very basically, the pursuer (person raising the court action) will lodge a written document with the court setting out the basis of their case: the facts they are relying on; the points in law that they want to make and the remedies they seek from the court (this is referred to as an Initial writ or petition). The defender will then lodge written defences, answering the points made by the pursuer and stating their counter arguments, both on points of fact and points of law. If the facts are disputed then a court hearing, called a proof, will be held. For this both sides must collect evidence.

Criminal
In criminal cases, the police will carry out an investigation, and will report to the procurator fiscal's department. The procurator fiscal will then decide whether to begin court action against the suspect. On beginning court action, the accused person is served with a Citation requiring them to appear in court on a specified date. On receipt of a citation, an accused person should seek legal advice. If the accused person pleads guilty, then the court can move to sentence the accused without having to hold a trial. However if the accused pleads not guilty, then the case will move towards trial. At this stage both sides will begin to collect their evidence.

1.31   Evidence
Evidence is the information that tends to prove or disprove the existence of a particular fact or set of facts. The courts look to the evidence to draw an inference as to the greater degree of probability of alleged events.

1.310   Burden and Standard of Proof
Generally a party who asserts a particular state of facts must prove them - this is referred to as the burden or onus of proof.The extent to which the party must prove their case is referred to as the Standard of Proof.

Civil

The burden of proof will switch between the parties depending on which party is relying on the facts at issue. The standard to which a party must prove their points is *the balance of probabilities.* Therefore anything more probable than not is treated as certain.

Criminal

The accused is presumed innocent until proven guilty, so the burden of proof lies with the Crown. Also, as they are presumed innocent, the standard of proof required is higher - *beyond reasonable doubt.* Any reasonable doubt at the end of the trial must be exercised in favour of the accused.

1.311   Presumptions

The burden, or duty to prove, can be shifted to the other party because of a legal presumption. A presumption is an inference from one fact of the probable existence of another fact.Some presumptions can be overridden by other evidence, such as:*pater est qui nuptiae demonstrant* - means that where a married woman gives birth to a child her husband is presumed to be the father. Whereas, there are some presumptions that are conclusive, that cannot be overridden, such as: A girl under the age of 12 cannot consent to sexual intercourse

1.312   Types of Evidence

1. Documentary

Written/ printed matter expressed in words, drawings etc. Apart from documents that have been signed by the granter in the presence of a witness, all other written material presented to the court may require to be spoken to by witnesses.

1.3120 Writing reports.

As reports and records written at any time could be essential in any court action to both sides, great care should be taken in report writing and record keeping. In addition to being mindful of NMC guidelines, the recorder of information should consider how they could explain to the court what happened. If a chart has been ticked but no more, who would know that the tick was theirs, and what exactly they had checked?The key information such as persons present, time, actions taken, should be recorded/ reported.

The quicker a report is written after the event in question, the better chance of accuracy. A report writer should only include information that they can verify or if relying on another, this should be noted.

1.3121 Ordering the Production of Documents.

There exists a process to enable a party to get documents that are either held by the other side or by some other body. The court will only order production of documents that appear necessary to answer questions that are likely to be raised in existing court action or action that is likely to be brought. This process is referred to as commission and diligence.If documents are required under a commission and diligence then they must be delivered to the other side, unless it is to be argued that the documents are protected under some legal privilege. Within the NHS, perhaps the most important privilege is that of Communications *post litem motam.* Literally means after an action has been raised. The general principle here is that parties should be free to prepare for litigation without the threat that the other side can through a commission and diligence access their work. So generally this would prevent the NHS having to pass over a report on the medical health of a patient carried out for the purpose of defending a claim for damages due to negligence.

2. Real

Actual physical things such as items of clothing, referred to as labels/ productions. A witness with first hand knowledge of the items must normally speak to real evidence

3. Oral
Witnesses - most important.

General: All witnesses who can give intelligible evidence are competent (allowed to give evidence) and all competent witnesses are compellable, that is can be required to give evidence. There is no longer a requirement for a child or person with mental incapacity to satisfy the court that they understand the difference between truth and lies before being allowed to give evidence. For witnesses who are deaf or unable to communicate due to physical or mental disability, an interpreter may be used. A witness will only become incompetent if they are totally unable to communicate. To make the whole experience less daunting for children often the Sheriff will remove his wig; clear the court of unnecessary personnel; and come down to the same level of the child. The Vulnerable Witnesses (Scotland) Act 2004 gives children under 16 and persons with mental disorder the right to special measures to assist them to give evidence.

The Scottish Executive has published the following information for witnesses:

http://www.scotland.gov.uk/Publications/2005/07/07105526/55283
Being a Witness for Children in Criminal Proceedings

http://www.scotland.gov.uk/Publications/2005/06/28154343/43454
Being a Witness for Young People in Criminal Proceedings

http://www.scotland.gov.uk/Publications/2005/06/2984605/46120
Being a Witness for Children in Children's Hearing Proceedings

http://www.scotland.gov.uk/Publications/2005/06/28141320/13224
Being a Witness for Young People in Children's Hearing Proceedings

http://www.scotland.gov.uk/Publications/2005/06/27110833/08419
Your Child is a Witness – A Booklet for Parents and Carers

http://www.scotland.gov.uk/Publications/2005/06/03104253/42547
Guidance on Special Measures for Vulnerable Child and Adult Witnesses

http://www.scotland.gov.uk/Publications/2007/11/22120443/0
A Guide to the Vulnerable Witnesses (Scotland) Act 2004

1.313 Role of a Witness
There is a checklist for those called as witnesses in Appendix One.

A person is called as a witness if either party is of the opinion that they may be able to provide evidence that is relevant to the case. A witness can be asked to give evidence of anything they themselves experienced through any of their senses, such as smell, hearing, and sight.

Opinion Evidence
In general, a witness is only to give evidence on the facts they observed, they are not entitled to give their opinion. However, if a witness has been called as an expert witness it is their role to give their opinion on matters within their expertise, although the court is not bound to accept their evidence.

Civil
A witness may give hearsay evidence. Hearsay evidence is not evidence of something that the witness said/ experienced themselves, rather it is evidence of something that they heard/ discovered from another source. It is therefore second hand, and as such is less reliable, so will be admitted by the court only "for what it is worth" - i.e. the court will decide what weight is to be given to that evidence.

Criminal

Hearsay evidence is not normally admissible, unless for example, the witness who would have given the evidence is now deceased.

Sometimes a witness will not be keen to disclose all information because they may have received that information in confidence. Generally the duty to the court overrules any other confidentiality, although in law some special protection is given to some professionals. Legal Professional Privilege prevents a solicitor from disclosing communications between them and their client. This ensures that accused persons can consult their solicitor frankly without fear of injuring any case that they may have.

1.314 Writing Reports and Appearing as a Witness in Private Law Cases

If a health professional is asked to write a report for a party in a private law case, e.g. a dispute about parental responsibilities and rights, they cannot be compelled to produce such a report. In a public law case, e.g. child protection, a report would have to be produced.If a health professional is asked to write a report or to appear as a witness in a private law case, they should consider very carefully whether this might be a breach of their professional code of confidentiality and whether it might adversely affect their ability to continue working effectively with the family in question. If the health professional thinks that it is inappropriate to write a report or appear as a witness in a private law case, they should make this clear to the requesting solicitor. If cited to appear as a witness, it is a requirement to appear in court.

1.32 Appearing as a Witness in Court

Appearing in court can be a daunting prospect, hence the special arrangements that may be made for child witnesses. Although a witness may be called to give evidence by one side, justice and fairness requires that the other side also have the opportunity to question the witness. Therefore before the court date it is likely that the legal teams acting for each side will contact all witnesses to get their statements.

On the date of the hearing the witnesses are not permitted to sit in the court, rather they remain in the witness room until they are called. On entering the witness box, the witness will be administered the oath. The side that called the witness will lead with the questioning, to get the witness to recount to the court all that happened on the appropriate date(s). Thereafter, the other side will have an opportunity to ask questions, perhaps to verify what exactly the witnesses saw, or to contradict/ challenge the witness.

When the witness has completed his or her evidence, it is important that they do not discuss the case with anyone else. This also applies if the court adjourns part way through the evidence of the witness.

The Vulnerable Witnesses (Scotland) Act 2004 gives the right to special measures to assist the giving of evidence to:

- children under 16
- any adult where there is a significant risk that the quality of the evidence may be diminished because they are suffering from a mental disorder, or fear or distress in connection with giving evidence at the trial or hearing

In determining whether a person is a vulnerable witness the court shall take into account-

(a) the nature and circumstances of the alleged offence to which the proceedings relate,
(b) the nature of the evidence which the person is likely to give,
(c) the relationship (if any) between the person and the accused,
(d) the person's age and maturity,
(e) any behaviour towards the person on the part of -
    (i) the accused,
    (ii) members of the family or associates of the accused,
    (iii) any other person who is likely to be an accused or a witness in the proceedings, *and*
(f) such other matters, including-
    (i) the social and cultural background and ethnic origins of the person,
    (ii) the person's sexual orientation,
    (iii) the domestic and employment circumstances of the person,
(iv) any religious beliefs or political opinions of the person, and
(v) any physical disability or other physical impairment which the person has,

as appear to the court to be relevant.

A vulnerable witness under the age of 16 **shall** be entitled to at least one of the special measures listed below:

a)   Use of a television link
b)   Use of a screen
c)   Use of a supporter

Further special measures are available on application to the court for witnesses under 16 and vulnerable adult witnesses:

- Use of a live television link from another part of the court building or other place outwith that building
- Greater use of prior statements of vulnerable witnesses as evidence in chief (in criminal cases only)
- Taking of evidence by a commissioner
- Use of a screen
- Use of a supporter

Where no special measures are specified the court must be satisfied that this is the witness's wish and is appropriate. In the case of child witnesses, the views of the child and parent must be obtained and taken into account.

The special measures may also be used in combination where appropriate.

The Act requires a person citing a vulnerable witness to give at least 14 days notice to the court. The notice must specify which special measure the person believes is most appropriate and may ask the court to consider allowing no special measures for the witness. **If you are working with someone who may be a vulnerable witness, you may need to remind the Procurator Fiscal or the Reporter to the Children's Panel that consideration needs to be given to special measures.**

A child under 12 will not normally be required to give evidence in court where the offence is murder, culpable homicide, a sexual offence, serious assault or neglect.

1.33 Remedies

Once all evidence and legal argument is heard the judge may make their decision. Often this is delivered immediately, however in some cases the judge will want to have time to reflect on the matter before giving their opinion. Their opinion, in writing, will be delivered at a later date. The whole point of taking a case to court is to get the court to grant a particular remedy. The following remedies are possible in Scottish cases:

Civil

- Damages - this is the assessment by the court of monetary compensation for a party who has suffered some loss.
- Declarator - this is where the courts declare that a person has a particular right or that a particular set of circumstances exist e.g. declaration of parentage.
- Interdict - this remedy is granted to prevent the continuation of a legal wrong or to prevent a legal wrong from occurring. May be granted in cases of domestic violence, to prevent the violent party from approaching the other.
- In addition to the above other remedies that may be granted include administrative matters such as the appointment of a financial guardian to an adult with incapacity or remedies such as divorce.

Criminal

Criminal sentences can easily be divided into:

- custodial sentences
- community based sentences such as probation and community service
- fines.
- Additionally the criminal court may decide to admonish the offender or to grant them an absolute discharge.

Custodial sentences comprise either imprisonment or for those under 18, detention in a young offenders institution.

The length of imprisonment will depend on the seriousness of the offences, the maximum power of the court and the accused's previous record of convictions

Fines. For many offences the court may decide that the appropriate punishment is a fine. Often the fine will be spread into frequent, smaller payments to avoid undue hardship. In addition to a fine, the court could also impose a Compensation Order requiring the accused to pay for property that they damaged.

Alternatively the court may decide to impose a sentence such as Community Service or Probation. Probation has the advantage of placing the accused under a degree of supervision, giving them the chance to prove to the court that they are capable of remaining out of trouble and providing support to deal with a significant underlying issue such as drugs or alcohol.

Sometimes the court will impose a Deferred Sentence until a specified date. This may be to give time for reports such as social Enquiry reports to be prepared by social work, to be produced to help them assess the best type of sentence, or merely to give the accused time to prove that they can remain trouble free (but without the supervision that accompanies probation).

1.4   Tribunals and other Bodies

Within the Scottish Legal System the power to decide on some issues has been given to bodies other than the courts, often to tribunals. Perhaps the most obvious are The Children's Panel - which deals with children in need of care or protection (see Part 4) or the Employment tribunal, which deals with employment issues. Generally the decision of these tribunals can be referred into the courts on disputed matters of law. As well as tribunals, which act as judicial forums, powers can also be given to other bodies to monitor practice in certain areas.

1.40   NMC

Within nursing, legal power has been given, since 1979, by the Nurses, Midwives and Health Visitor Acts to the NMC (formerly the UKCC) to protect the interests of the public. The NMC carries out this role in two ways.

- It maintains a register of those who are suitable practitioners and exercises powers to remove persons from the register if they are either seriously ill or have had a charge of misconduct proven against them.

- It publishes The Code of Professional Conduct, thereby defining the responsibilities of practitioners and the conduct expected of them. The importance of the NMC Code will be seen in Chapters 2 and 6.

1.41   Professional Conduct Complaints

The NMC is only concerned with an allegation of either misconduct or serious illness that poses a risk to the public. Therefore if a person who is seriously ill withdraws from practice, the NMC will not get involved. Similarly if the misconduct alleged does not put patients at risk/ seriously affect patient care, the NMC will not get involved.

1.42   Preliminary Proceedings Committee (PPC)

The Preliminary Proceedings Committee (PPC) screens any allegation of misconduct. The PPC may decide to take no action, issue a formal caution (which remains on the NMC register for 5 years) or to refer the matter either to the Professional Conduct Committee or (in cases alleging serious illness) to the Panel of Screeners for the Health Committee. If the matter is being referred, an interim suspension could be made if in the circumstances to allow the practitioner to continue would expose patients to a high risk. Interim suspensions are reviewed every three months

1.43   Professional Conduct Committee (PCC)

The Professional Conduct Committee sits as a panel of usually five and it holds its hearings in public. Due to the court nature of this hearing, legal representation is permitted. Often this will be arranged through a trade union. As it is dealing with the issue of whether serious misconduct has been proven, it operates on the same principles as the criminal courts. Therefore cases must be proven beyond reasonable doubt.If the facts are not proven, or are deemed not to amount to serious misconduct no further action would be taken.If the case is proven, the PCC may issue a caution, may remove the practitioner from the register either for a specified period of time or indefinitely, or may refer to the Health Committee (if serious ill health is involved)Any person removed from the register may apply to be restored to it. However the applications will not be heard unless the time specified has expired, or in the case of indefinite removal not normally until 12 months have expired from the date of removal.

1.44   The General Medical Council (GMC)

The General Medical Council (GMC) was established under the Medical Act of 1858, with legal powers designed to maintain the standards the public have a right to expect of doctors. Where any doctor fails to meet those standards, the GMC can protect patients from harm - if necessary, by striking the doctor off the register and removing their right to practise medicine.

The governing body of the GMC, the Council, has 35 members:
- 19 doctors elected by the doctors on the register;
- 14 members of the public appointed by the Privy Council;
- 2 academics appointed by educational bodies - the universities and medical royal colleges.

The GMC has powers to:
- prevent a doctor from practising;
- suspend a doctor from the register; *or*
- place conditions on their registration.

It can also issue a warning when satisfied that there is no need to use the powers above.

The GMC can only take action against doctors. These include hospital doctors and general practitioners, whether in the NHS or private practice.

It can take formal action if the doctor has:
- behaved badly/inappropriately;
- not done their job properly;
- a criminal conviction or caution in the British Isles or elsewhere;
- been found guilty by another regulatory body whether in the British Isles or overseas; *or*
- where the doctor's fitness to practise is impaired due to physical or mental ill health.

It can also issue a warning where there has been a significant departure from the standards set out in the GMC Guidance or a performance assessment has highlighted a significant cause for concern.

GMC procedures are divided into two distinct stages:

- investigation, where the GMC will assess whether or not it needs to further consider if the doctor is fit to practise; *and*
- adjudication, that comprises a hearing (normally in public) before a Fitness To Practice Panel.

If there is evidence that patients may be at risk, the GMC can suspend or restrict a doctor's registration as an interim measure.

Part One - Appendix 1
Checklist for Witnesses

Evidence
- Is it a civil or a criminal case?
- The standard of proof in a criminal case is higher (beyond reasonable doubt) than the standard of proof in a civil case (on the balance of probabilities);
- You may be asked to give a precognition to the legal representative for the opposing side. This is to establish what evidence you are likely to be able to give;
- Your evidence must be relevant;
- Hearsay evidence (repeating what someone said) is permitted in civil cases, but only under very exceptional circumstances in criminal cases;
- You cannot refuse to answer questions on the grounds of a professional duty of confidentiality.

Preparation
- You will usually be an ordinary witness, not an expert;
- Ordinary witnesses give factual evidence;
- Expert witnesses may give opinion evidence;
- **Check where and when you are required to appear;**
- **Check with the person calling you as a witness what they expect of you;**
- **Refresh your memory before your day in court (is your record keeping adequate, bearing in mind that you may be coming to court many months after an event?);**
- Do you need to take notes into the witness box? If yes, check with the person calling you as a witness;
- Do not take documents into the witness box that have not been notified to the court in advance;
- Make sure you are dressed in a way that shows respect to the court;
- Make sure that you have your glasses, if you need them.

In Court
- Take the oath or affirm (promise to tell the truth);
- Stand up to give your evidence unless you are offered the chance to sit;
- Give name, age and professional address;
- Speak slowly and clearly (the Sheriff needs to take notes);
- Examination-in-chief (questions from the person who called you as a witness);
- Cross-examination (by the opposing legal representative);
- Re-examination (by the person who called you as a witness to clarify any final points arising from cross-examination);
- Take time to think before answering questions;
- Ask for a question to be repeated;
- Answer confidently, accurately and with clarity;
- Stick to the question asked;
- Keep calm. Cross-examination may be fairly aggressive and challenging;
- Ask for a break, if you need one;
- Address the sheriff or judge as My Lord or My Lady.

Credibility
You must be a credible witness. Credibility is about:
- How you are dressed;
- Do you conduct yourself in a professional manner?
- Do you answer questions confidently and accurately?
- Does the court believe you?

After You Have Given Your Evidence
Do not discuss your evidence with anyone else. This also applies if the court adjourns before you have completed your evidence.

Part Two
Data Protection, Confidentiality, Human Rights & Information Sharing

Part Two

Data Protection, Confidentiality, Human Rights & Information Sharing

2.0   Introduction

By necessity, nursing requires patients to disclose an amount of information about them. It is very important to the patient/ nurse relationship, that a patient has confidence that the information will not being used for any other purpose, than their treatment. Such an expectation is highlighted in the *Patient's Charter and You*, which states *"everyone working for the NHS is under a legal duty to keep your records confidential"*

Information, which is confidential, is essentially protected in three ways.
- by a general duty of confidentiality, including professional codes of practice;
- by the Data Protection Act 1998, covering information which has been recorded and stored, such as computer and written records;
- by the Human Rights Act 1998 Article 8 the right to respect for private life.

However, confidentiality is never an absolute right and the law and the professional codes recognise that there will be legitimate circumstances where confidentiality may be breached.

2.1   General Duty of Confidentiality

Breach of confidence can give rise to a claim in the civil courts for damages. Such an action is likely to be taken if an employee were to disclose confidential information about their employer. Disclosure of confidential information can, however, be permitted 'in the public interest'.

Public interest requires the disclosure by the police of certain information concerning sex offenders, and more generally, disclosing information necessary for the purposes of preventing, detecting or exposing a crime. The disclosure of information gained in the course of employment is permitted in certain circumstances by the Public Interest Disclosure Act 1998. It applies where it appears it is likely that the one of the following has occurred and is being or is likely to be concealed:

- that a criminal offence has occurred;
- that a person has failed, is failing or is likely to fail to comply with any legal obligation;
- that a miscarriage of justice has occurred, is occurring or is likely to occur;
- that the health or safety of any individual has been, is being or is likely to be endangered;
- that the environment has been, is being or is likely to be damaged, or
- that information tending to show any matter falling into any of the above categories has been or is likely to be deliberately concealed.

2.2   Moral/ Professional Issues

The NMC Code of Professional Conduct, in Clause 10 places a duty on all nurses and midwives that they must
"protect all confidential information concerning patients and clients obtained in the course of professional practice and make disclosures only with consent, where required by the order of a court or where you can justify disclosure in the wider public interest."

The GMC Code states that doctors should:
- Seek patients' consent to disclosure of information wherever possible;
- Anonymise data where unidentifiable data will serve the purpose;
- Keep disclosures to the minimum necessary;
- Be prepared to justify decisions in accordance with the guidance.

If the patient withholds consent, or consent cannot be obtained, disclosures may be made only where they can be justified in the public interest, usually where disclosure is essential to protect the patient, or someone else, from risk of death or serious harm.

The new SSSC Code applicable to social care workers issued in 2002 states that they must:

- Respect confidential information and clearly explain agency policies about confidentiality to services users and carers.

2.3   Disclosure without consent

On a need to know basis - the patient should be made aware that certain information would be shared with other health care professionals in the course of planning treatment;

- It may be required by the order of a court *or*
- It may occur where you can justify disclosure in the wider public interest. The decision remains with the individual nurse as to whether they are of the opinion that public interest justifies the disclosure of information without patient consent. Should it appear necessary to release information, guidance should be sought from the NMC or a colleague and in terms of NMC standards for Records and Record Keeping, a record of the reasons for disclosure should be noted and kept - it may be required at a later date to explain/ justify the action taken.

In addition some types of information must be disclosed to other health officials. The Public Health (Notification of Infectious Diseases) (Scotland) Regulations 1988 require the notification of a patient suffering from the diseases listed in Regulations to the Chief Medical officer.

2.4   The Data Protection Act 1998

This Act updated the law regulating the processing of information relating to individuals, replacing the Data Protection Act 1984. It covers:

- The rules about the obtaining, use, storage and sharing of information;
- The right of access to information by the data subject;
- The rules about security of information.

It applies to computer and paper files.

The whole system is monitored through the Information Commissioner, whose responsibility it is to maintain a register of those persons/ companies (referred to in the Act as a "data controller") who have notified him that they are processing personal data. Any data controller who processes information without notification to the Commissioner is guilty of an offence.

The Commissioner also has a role in ensuring that data controllers observe the general principles of data protection which are specified in the Act.

2.40   The Data Protection Principles

1. **Personal data shall be obtained and processed fairly and lawfully.**
    This means that the data subject should know that you are obtaining information about him or her, how that information will be used and with whom it may be shared.

    At least one of these conditions must be met:

    *   the data subject has given consent;
    *   processing is necessary for the performance of a contract with the data subject;
    *   processing is necessary to comply with a legal requirement;
    *   processing is necessary to protect the vital interests of the data subject;
    *   processing is necessary for the administration of justice;
    *   processing is necessary in pursuit of the legitimate interests of the data controller.

    In addition, if the data is "sensitive", i.e. relates to racial or ethnic origin, political opinions, religion, trade union membership, physical or mental health, sexuality, or criminal offences, at least one of the following conditions must also apply:

    *   the data subject has given consent;
    *   processing is necessary in relation to employment law;
    *   processing is necessary to protect the vital interests of the data subject;

- processing is necessary in relation to legal advice or legal proceedings;
- processing is necessary in relation to the administration of justice;
- processing is necessary in relation to the health of the data subject and is undertaken by a health professional of other person with a similar duty of confidentiality;
- processing is necessary in relation to equal opportunities.

This covers lawful processing. For fair processing, the data subject must be aware that personal information is being stored and the purpose.

2. **Data may only be held for one or more specified and lawful purposes.** The specified purpose(s) will be those specified in the notification to the Information Commissioner.

3. **Data must be adequate, relevant and not excessive for the purpose.**

4. **Data must be accurate, and if not, must be amended and kept up to date.**

5. **Data must not be kept for longer than necessary.**

6. **Personal data must be processed in accordance with the rights of the data subject.**
    - **The right to have data corrected;**
    - **The right to stop processing if it would cause damage or distress;**
    - **The right to have access to the data, subject to certain exceptions. A request must be made in writing to the data controller who may charge up to £10 and must reply within 40 days.**

7. **Data must be secure and there must be no unauthorized access, alteration, disclosure to third parties or accidental loss.**

This means that you must keep your paper and computer files secure, whether in your place of work or elsewhere, if you have to take files away from the workplace. You must also be careful about sharing information. Either you should have consent to do this or you can objectively justify it.

Unlawful disclosure is a criminal offence.

8.   Transfer of data outside the European Economic Area is restricted.

2.41   Gaining Access to Information

Where an individual discovers that any person/ organisation holds personal data, which they are going to process, the individual can make a written request to be provided with a description of:

- the personal data being held;
- the purpose for which they are being processed;
- the recipients or classes of recipients to whom the information may be disclosed.

Moreover, the individual can request that they be given, in an intelligible form:

- information containing any personal information, and the source of that information;
- where the information has been processed automatically for evaluation purposes, such as creditworthiness, the logic involved in the decision taking.

The data subject is entitled to a written copy of the information held about him or her.

The data controller may refuse to release information if:

- the request is not made in writing or the correct fee is not paid;
- they are not satisfied as to the identity of the person making the request or have not received enough information to locate the data;
- to comply to the request would involve disclosing information relating to another individual, unless that individual has consented to the releasing of the information, or in all the circumstances it is reasonable to release the information without that person's consent.

Once an individual has received the information above they can take action to prevent the data being processed for a variety of purposes such as direct marketing, automated decision taking or other processing likely to cause damage or distress.

In the event that the data controller fails to comply either with their request for information or to cease processing the information, they can raise civil court proceedings against the data controller. These rights apply to any person who is of sufficient age and maturity. Young persons from the age of 12 are deemed to have sufficient maturity.

2.42   Control Over Disclosure of Information

Normally, the data subject or someone acting legally on his or her behalf, must consent to the sharing of information, unless it is

- required by law *or*
- justified in the public interest *or*
- for the prevention or detection of crime *or*
- necessary in the vital interests of the data subject.

The Data Protection Act adds to the general common law provisions on the disclosure of information. Essentially where a data controller holds information it is an offence for that information to be disclosed without the consent of the data controller to a third party. This is to prevent employees misusing their access to information. The general exceptions to non-disclosure such as it being necessary to prevent crime or disclosure being required by order of court apply.

The Act also protects individuals from disclosure of their personal data. It prevents companies and other persons including in their standard contract conditions that allow them to obtain data from specified third parties. It is not possible to require the Police to provide data on an individual's criminal convictions. Similarly any contractual term which seeks to require an individual to provide their health record, whether in whole or in part, or a copy of such records, is legally void, unenforceable. This covers all records made by a health professional (which is broadly defined and includes medical practitioners, dentists, nurses, midwives and health visitors). The principle here is to prevent individuals being forced, perhaps by potential employers, to use their rights to access data held on them, for use by the employer.

2.43   Access to Medical Records Under the Data Protection Act 1998

Patients have a right to access their medical records **subject to certain exceptions**. A person may be denied access to **parts** of his health records

- if it would be cause serious harm to that person or to another individual
  or
- if it would identify a third party other than a health professional involved in his care.

The law makes it clear that refusal of access will be exceptional. Such a decision must therefore be taken only after consultation with a senior medical professional.

Where access to a record is refused, the nurse, midwife or health professional should record their reasons for refusal. This enables justification of the decision at a later date.

In response to an application for access, the individual should obtain access to the record. The access sought can be to inspect the records, to obtain copies of records, in whole or in part, or to supply a copy with an explanation (in cases where without an explanation the record would be unintelligible). Where access is denied, the patient who is aggrieved may complain to the appropriate Health Board or Trust. If the applicant is still dissatisfied they may apply to the civil court to order access.

Once a patient has received access to health records they have the ability to apply to the holder of the record to have any inaccuracy amended. An inaccuracy refers to anything that is incorrect, misleading or incomplete. The holder of the record may either amend the record if they are satisfied that it was inaccurate, or make a note on the record of those matters that the patient disputes as inaccurate. The patient should be provided with a copy of either the amended record or note, without charge.

Parental Access to a Child's Health Record
Where a child has sufficient maturity to give informed consent or refusal, parents may only access the child's health record with the consent of the child. In addition, only a parent with parental responsibilities and rights may normally access the record, if the child is unable to give consent.

2.44 Access to Social Work Records Under the Data Protection Act 1998

Access to parts of these records may be denied if

- it would cause serious harm to the physical or mental health of the client or any other person *or*
- if a third party would be identified, unless that person is a social work professional.

A person acting on behalf of a child or an adult with incapacity may not have access to the following information:

- information disclosed by the data subject in the expectation that it would not be disclosed to that person;
- information obtained from any examination or investigation to which the data subject consented, in the expectation that it would not be disclosed;
- information which the data subject expressly stated should not be disclosed.

Where a social work record contains health information, it may not be disclosed without first consulting the appropriate health professional, **but the final decision about disclosure rests with the social work department.**

2.45 Records That May Not Be Accessed Under the Data Protection Act 1998

The Act does not allow access to

- information supplied by the Reporter to the Children's Panel for the purpose of a Hearing;
- adoption records (dealt with under The Adoption (S) Act 1978);
- information about a child's special educational needs (dealt with under The Education (Additional Support for Learning) (S) Act 2004).

2.5   Access to Medical Records Act 1990

The Access to Medical Records Act 1990 now only applies to applications to access the files of a deceased person. Applications from living individuals are now dealt with under The Data Protection Act 1998 which gives access to the whole record, rather than records made since 1st November 1991.

2.6   Human Rights and The Right to Respect for Private Life

The Human Rights Act 1998 applies to all public authorities and makes it unlawful for a public authority to act or to fail to act in a manner inconsistent with the rights set out in the European Convention on Human Rights.

Article 8 states that:
1. *Everyone has the right to respect for his private and family life, his home and his correspondence.*
2. *There shall be no interference by a public authority with the exercise of this right except such as is in accordance with the law and is necessary in a democratic society in the interests of national security, public safety or the economic well-being of the country, for the prevention of disorder or crime, for the protection of health or morals, or for the protection of the rights and freedoms of others.*

Professionals must therefore
- Have proper regard to the terms of their code and the general law on confidentiality, including Article 8 and the Data Protection Act 1998;
- Show that they are pursuing a legitimate aim (e.g. protection from significant harm);
- Have sufficient and relevant reasons to justify their interference with the right to respect for private life;
- Show that they have acted proportionately.

Failure to protect an individual may also be a breach of their human rights.
A person who believes that his or her human rights have been breached may bring a case against the public authority to a civil court within 12 months of the alleged breach. Compensation may be awarded if the breach is proved. The victim of the breach may also report the breach to the professional body.

2.7 Information Sharing in Relation to Child Protection

2.70 The Data Protection Act 1998

The Data Protection Act 1998 states that data must be secure and there must be no unauthorised access, alteration, disclosure to third parties or accidental loss. Unlawful disclosure is a criminal offence, but the Act does **not** prevent sharing of information if someone is at significant risk of harm

In broad terms, the Act and accompanying regulations allow for information to be disclosed (or held) **even without an individual's consent** where it is necessary:

- For the prevention or detection of crime;
- For the exercise of public functions carried out in the public interest;
- For the protection of the vital interests of the data subject.

2.71 Human Rights and Privacy

The Human Rights Act 1998 applies to all public authorities and makes it unlawful for a public authority to act or to fail to act in a manner inconsistent with the rights set out in the European Convention on Human Rights.

Article 8 states that:

- Everyone has the right to respect for his private and family life, his home and his correspondence.
- There shall be no interference by a public authority with the exercise of this right except such as is in accordance with the law and is necessary in a democratic society in the interests of national security, public safety or the economic well-being of the country, for the prevention of disorder or crime, for the protection of health or morals, or for the protection of the rights and freedoms of others.

Professionals must therefore

- Have proper regard to the terms of their code and the general law on confidentiality, including Article 8 and the Data Protection Act 1998.
- Show that they are pursuing a legitimate aim (e.g. protection from significant harm).
- Have sufficient and relevant reasons to justify their interference with the right to respect for private life.
- Show that they have acted proportionately.

Failure to protect an individual may also be a breach of their human rights.

2.72   Confidentiality – Professional Codes

The code issued by the **NMC** in 2002 states that registered nurses and midwives must protect confidential information and use it only for the purpose for which it was given. Patients and clients must be made aware that information may have to be shared and their consent should be sought at the outset for such information sharing. **Confidentiality may only be breached in the public interest or if required by law.**

The code issued by the **GMC** in 2000 states that doctors should:
- Seek patients' consent to disclosure of information wherever possible;
- Anonymise data where unidentifiable data will serve the purpose;
- Keep disclosures to the minimum necessary;
- Be prepared to justify decisions in accordance with the guidance.

If the patient withholds consent, or consent cannot be obtained, disclosures may be made only where they can be justified in the public interest, usually where disclosure is essential to protect the patient, or someone else, from risk of death or serious harm.

The new **SSSC** Code applicable to social care workers issued in 2002 states that they must:

Respect confidential information and clearly explain agency policies about confidentiality to services users and carers

Confidentiality is not absolute and professionals must balance the right to confidentiality with their duty of care.

2.73 Extracts from Guidance on Information Sharing From the Scottish Executive (2004) http://www.scotland.gov.uk/library5/health/sicr-00.asp

All professionals and agencies are required to keep confidential information given to them during the course of their work. Information given to professionals by their patient, client or service user should not be shared with others without the person's permission, unless the safety of the person or other vulnerable people may otherwise be put at risk. This general principle is enshrined in professional and ethical codes of conduct, and in human rights and data protection legislation, which acknowledge an individual's right to privacy but which also enable the disclosure and sharing of information in appropriate circumstances.

Agencies beginning work with families should explain their policy on information sharing and confidentiality carefully, and help parents and, where appropriate, children and young people, to understand the circumstances under which information may have to be shared with others without their consent.

If there is reasonable concern that a child may be at risk of harm this will always override a professional or agency requirement to keep information confidential. All professionals and service providers have a responsibility to act to make sure that a child whose safety or welfare may be at risk is protected from harm. They should always tell parents this.

When any professional or agency approaches another to ask for information they should be able to explain:

- what kind of information they need;
- why they need it;
- what they will do with the information; and
- who else may need to be informed, if concerns about a child persist.

All professionals and agencies should keep clear, legible and up-to-date records of:

- contact with parents and children;
- what information is held and any consent by parents or children to information being shared with other agencies or professionals;
- the assessment, care plan and any changes as a result of reviews of these and;
- contact with other agencies, including the date and content of information shared or discussions held.

Records should be dated and should identify the person recording the information. Agencies should comply with the principles of data protection legislation and guidance.

2.74 Recording

The Data Protection Act 1998 states that data must be adequate, relevant and not excessive for the purpose.

The NMC advise that as a registered nurse, midwife or health visitor, you have both a professional and a legal duty of care. Your record keeping should therefore be able to demonstrate:

- a full account of your assessment and the care you have planned and provided;
- relevant information about the condition of the patient or client at any given time;
- measures you have taken to respond to their needs;
- evidence that you have understood and honoured your duty of care, that you have taken all reasonable steps to care for the patient or client and that any actions or omissions on your part have not compromised their safety in any way;
- a record of any arrangements you have made for the continuing care of a patient or client.

The frequency of entries will be determined both by your professional judgement and local standards and agreements.

Part Three
Family Law

Part Three
Family Law

3.1   Parentage

The woman who carries the child (irrespective of biological connection) is in law the mother of the child. **(Human Fertilisation and Embryology Act 1990).**

The father must in law be biologically related to the child. There are 2 legal presumptions to help in situations where there is uncertainty about the father:-

- if the mother is married, her husband is presumed to be the father of the child, if he is married to the mother at any time between conception and birth;
- if the mother is not married, a man is presumed to be the father, if he has accepted the child and is recorded as the father on the child's birth certificate.
(Section 5 Law Reform (Parent and Child) (S) Act 1986.)

If there is a dispute about the identity of the father, it is possible to apply to the court for a *declarator of parentage* which declares the identity of the father, based on DNA evidence.

3.2   Parental Responsibilities and Rights

The Children (S) Act 1995
Parents have the responsibility to:

- safeguard and promote the child's health, development and welfare;
- provide direction and guidance to the child;
- maintain personal relations and direct contact with the child;
- act as the child's legal representative;

Responsibilities end at 16, except the responsibility to give guidance which continues to 18.

Parents have the right to:

- have the child living with them or regulate the child's residence;
- control, direct and guide the child;
- maintain personal relations and direct contact with the child;
- act as the child's legal representative;

Parental rights end at 16.

3.20   Who has parental responsibilities and rights?

Mothers always have parental responsibilities and rights, **but a father only has them automatically if he is married to the mother at date of conception of the child or at any time subsequently. (Section 3)**

The natural father may acquire them by signing an agreement with the mother which must be registered in the official registers in Edinburgh. **(Section 4)**

The natural father and any person who can show an interest in the child may apply to the court for parental responsibilities and rights. **(Section 11)**

The Family Law (Scotland) Act 2006 changed the law so that if an unmarried father is named on the birth certificate on or after 4th May 2006, he will automatically have parental responsibilities and rights. Fathers named on the birth certificate prior to 4th May 2006 will not have automatic responsibilities and rights under the Children (Scotland) Act 1995.

3.21   The court may grant the following orders:

- **Residence Order** - regulates where the child lives up to age 16;

- **Contact Order** - regulates who may have contact with the child up to age 16;

- **Specific Issue Order** - regulates one specific issue in connection with parental responsibilities and rights, e.g. medical consent;

- **Interdict** - an order prohibiting the exercise of parental responsibilities and rights in a particular way;

- **An order depriving a person of parental responsibilities and rights** - note that there is no automatic loss of responsibilities and rights, they have to be removed by the court;

- **Appointment of a guardian** - a person to stand in for a parent who has died. The guardian will have full parental responsibilities and rights.

Note: a parent with parental responsibilities and rights may appoint a guardian to act after the death of the parent, but the appointment must be **in writing and signed by the parent.** This appointment would commence automatically on the death of the parent.

Courts dealing with cases involving parental responsibilities and rights must take into account the **3 overarching principles of The Children (S) Act 1995:-**

- the welfare of the child is paramount;
- the child must be given an opportunity to express a view and that view must be taken into consideration;
- no order must be made unless it benefits the child.

The Family Law (S) Act 2006 amended section 11 of the 1995 Act, so that the courts must take into account any abuse or risk of abuse that has affected or might affect the child.

3.22   Who can give consent for a child?
For a summary of the law in relation to consent to treatment for all age groups see Part Six.

Under **The Age of Legal Capacity (S) Act 1991** a child under 16 may give medical or dental consent if the medical practitioner treating the child deems the child able to understand the nature and consequences of the medical or dental procedure. If the child is competent to give consent or refusal, parental consent is irrelevant. If a child is too young to give consent, a person with parental responsibilities and rights may give such consent, acting as the child's legal representative.

In addition, under **Section 5 of The Children (S) Act 1995** a person with care or control of the child may give medical consent, if the child is too young and if that person is not aware that a parent would otherwise object.

3.23   At what age may a child appoint a solicitor?
Under **The Age of Legal Capacity (S) Act 1991** a child may appoint a solicitor at any age, if the child has a general understanding of what it means to do so. Children may claim legal aid in their own right, independent of the means of their parents.

3.24   Who must financially support a child?
Under **The Family Law (S) Act 1985** each parent and any person who has accepted the child as part of their family has a duty to financially support their child, irrespective of whether they have parental responsibilities and rights. This duty lasts to 18 or 25, if the child is in full time education. Financial support is decided by a court.

Under **The Child Support Act 1991** each parent has a duty to support their child up to age 16 or 19, if the child is in full time education. The Child Support Act takes precedence over The Family Law (S) Act. Financial support is decided by The Child Support Agency.

3.3   Marriage

A person may marry in Scotland at age 16. Parental consent is not required.

The legal consequences of marriage are:

- a duty to live together;
- a duty to financially support each other (even if separated) (known as aliment);
- a right to inherit after the death of the spouse as follows:-

if no will is left (intestate):

- house up to £300,000;

- furniture and fittings up to £24,000;
- cash sum of £42,000 (or £75,000 if there are no children);
- plus legal rights of one third of the moveable property (or one half if there are no children);
- If a will is left leaving everything to someone other than the spouse, the spouse would still get legal rights as above.

The Matrimonial Homes (Family Protection) (S) Act 1981

This Act deals with 2 issues:-

- it gives a spouse or civil partner automatic occupancy rights in the matrimonial home, even if that spouse or civil partner has no ownership in the property or is not named on the tenancy agreement. This means that a spouse or civil partner has the right to stay in the property or re-enter it at any time;

- it also allows for a spouse or civil partner to apply to the court to have an abusive partner excluded from the matrimonial home and for the spouse or civil partner to apply for interdicts (court orders) to prohibit abusive behaviour.

The Civil Partnership Act 2004

This Act provides for same sex partnerships to be registered and gives civil partners broadly the same rights as spouses.

3.4   Cohabiting Partners (including same sex partners)

Cohabiting partners have no duty to financially support each other and no right to inherit from a partner, unless that partner leaves a will in their favour. **The Family Law (S) Act 2006** makes provision for a cohabiting partner to apply to the court for a financial award on separation or on death. In the case of separation, the application must be made within 12 months and in the case of death, within 6 months. There is no automatic right to a financial award.

A cohabiting partner would have to apply to the court for occupancy rights, if that partner had no interest in the property. The cohabiting partner must acquire occupancy rights before an exclusion order may be applied for.

From December 2005 same sex couples who register a civil partnership will have the same legal rights and responsibilities as a married couple.
The term "common law wife/husband" has no legal meaning in Scotland. It is not possible to acquire the rights of a spouse by simply living together.

There is a form of common law marriage in Scotland known as marriage by cohabitation with habit and repute. It is possible for a couple to become married without going through a ceremony if they fulfil all of the following:-

- live together as husband and wife in Scotland for a sufficient period of time (unspecified);
- be generally regarded as husband and wife by those around them;
- have capacity to marry, i.e. not already married to someone else.

Before the authorities will recognise such a marriage, an application must be made to the Court of Session in Edinburgh for a *declarator of marriage* which would then allow for the marriage to be registered. This form of marriage is now being phased out.

3.5   Divorce

The Divorce (S) Act 1976
The grounds for divorce are as follows:

irretrievable breakdown of the marriage evidenced by:
- adultery;
- behaviour;
- non-cohabitation for 1 year and there is agreement to divorce;
- non-cohabitation for 2 years and no agreement is required.

The Family Law (S) Act 1985
This act makes the following provisions in relation to financial settlements on divorce:-
- matrimonial property should be shared fairly between the parties;

- economic advantage or disadvantage experienced by the parties should be taken into account;
- the economic burden of caring for a child under 16 should be shared equally;
- a person who has been substantially financially dependent on the other party should be awarded financial provision over no more than 3 years to allow for adjustment to the circumstances;
- a person who is likely to suffer extreme financial hardship as a result of the divorce should be awarded sufficient financial provision to relieve that hardship over a reasonable period of time.

In general, the law expects that as far as possible, there will be a clean break settlement.

3.6   Adoption

The Adoption (S) Act 1978

The Adoption (S) Act 1978 (is the legislation force as at February 2008 but the Adoption and Children (Scotland) Act 2007 will make changes to adoption law when brought into force.

Adoption is the severing of the legal relationship between child and natural parent or parents and the creation of a new legal relationship by the transferral of all parental responsibilities and rights to the adoptive parents.

Before a child may be adopted, the court must have the consent of each parent or guardian with parental responsibilities and rights. If consent cannot be obtained, there are a number of grounds upon which the court may dispense with the requirement for parental consent:-

- the parent is not known, cannot be found or is incapable of giving consent;
- the parent is withholding consent unreasonably;
- the parent has persistently failed without reasonable cause to fulfil parental responsibilities and rights in relation to the child;

- the parent has seriously ill-treated the child who is not likely to be reintegrated into the household **(Section 16).**

Under the 2007 Act the grounds will be:
- that the parent or guardian is dead,
- that the parent or guardian cannot be found or is incapable of giving consent,
- the parent is in the opinion of the court, unable satisfactorily to discharge parental responsibilities, or exercise parental rights rights, and is likely to continue to be unable to do so

The court must take into account the following **principles:-**

- the welfare of the child throughout life is paramount;
- the views of the child must be sought and taken into account;
- the child's racial, cultural, religious and linguistic background must be taken into account **(Section 6).**

A child aged 12 or over must also consent to his or her adoption.
A mother cannot consent to adoption in the first six weeks after the birth of the child.

3.60   Who can adopt?
There are no upper age limits, unless adoption agencies set their own.
In general, people under 21 cannot adopt.
Adopters must either be a married couple or a single person. **(Sections 14 and 15)**
Under the 2007 Act joint adoption by unmarried couples, including same sex couples will be permitted.

3.61   Who can be adopted?
The child must be under 18 and unmarried. **(Section 12)**

If the child is being adopted by a step-parent or relative or has been placed with adopters by an adoption agency, the child must be at least 19 weeks old and must have lived with the adopters for the previous 13 weeks before an adoption order can be granted.

If the child is being adopted by a non-relative and the child was not placed by an adoption agency, e.g. adoption by foster carers or adoption of a child from abroad, the child must be at least one year old and must have lived with the adopters for at least one year before the adoption order can be made. **(Section 13)**

3.62   What is freeing for adoption?

Only a local authority may apply to have a child freed for adoption.

Freeing is often used as a first step in the adoption process, in order to deal with the issue of consent at an early stage, rather than at the end of the process. It may be used where parents are consenting and wish to step out of the process as quickly as possible or where parents are withholding consent and the court is being asked to dispense with consent on the grounds already mentioned above.

Freeing for adoption transfers all parental responsibilities and rights to the local authority which then has to give consent for the final adoption.

Under the 2007 Act freeing for adoption ceases to exist.

Freeing for adoption and the parental responsibilities order will be replaced by the new permanence order, a court order which will regulate the exercise of parental responsibilities and parental rights in respect of children who cannot reside with their parents but where contact or shared exercise of parental responsibilities and parental rights is appropriate. A permanence order may remove certain parental responsibilities and parental rights and grant them to other parties specified in the order. Only a local authority may apply for a permanence order.

3.63   Court procedure

Most adoption applications are heard in the Sheriff Court.

The court appoints a *curator ad litem* and a *reporting officer.*

The curator is an independent person who must report to the court based on the welfare of the child. The reporting officer is required to obtain the consent of the natural parents, or, if they are not consenting, to report this to the court.

The role of the curator is similar to that of a safeguarder appointed by a children's hearing. A safeguarder investigates what is best for the child and makes recommendations to the hearing.

3.64 Access to records

A child may access his or her adoption records at age 16.

3.65 Intercountry adoption

The process of intercountry adoption begins with obtaining entry clearance from the Home Office to bring the child into the country. The Home Office will need to have the following information:

- Evidence of the child's identity;
- That the adoption is likely to be in the best interests of the child;
- The reasons for the proposed adoption;
- Background information on the child, including a medical report on the BAAF form;
- Evidence that there was permission for the child to leave his or her country for the purpose of adoption;
- Evidence that the authorities in that country will support the adoption;
- A valid parental agreement to the adoption or evidence that the child has been abandoned;
- That the prospective adopters are suitable to adopt the particular child.

3.7 Fostering

The Fostering of Children (S) Regulations 1996

A child may be placed with foster carers by the local authority in a variety of circumstances

- if the child is accommodated under Section 25 of The Children (S) Act 1995;
- if the child is placed on supervision by the Children's Panel under Section 70 of The Children (S) Act 1995;
- if the child is subject to a child protection order under Section 57 of The Children (S) Act 1995.

(For explanations of these child protection procedures, please refer to Part 4).

Foster carers do **not** automatically acquire parental responsibilities and rights, but as persons with care or control of the child under Section 5 of The Children (S) Act 1995, they would have the limited right to give medical consent, if the child was unable to give his or her own consent and if the foster carer is not aware that a parent would object. However, the local authority may restrict the right of foster carers to give such consent. Foster carers would then have to refer back to the local authority which might hold a blanket consent from the parents. If not, then the local authority must refer to parents to obtain consent.

3.70   Who may be approved as a foster carer?

A man and a woman living and acting together or a man or a woman living and acting alone.

Foster carers are approved by the local authority after a rigorous checking procedure. A foster carer may be approved for particular children or for any child. Approval must be reviewed annually.

3.71   Placing a child

The local authority may not place a child with foster carers unless they have been approved and the placement is in the child's best interest and the foster carers have entered into a written agreement.

In an emergency, a child may be placed with an approved foster carer for up to 72 hours with a limited written agreement, but the full agreement must be signed before the end of the emergency period, if the placement is to continue.

A child may be placed with a relative or friend who is not an approved foster carer for up to 6 weeks, if the local authority is satisfied that the placement is in the child's best interests. This is used to prevent the child from having to stay with strangers, when the child needs to be removed form home. If the placement is to continue beyond 6 weeks, the carers would have to be approved, unless the Children's Panel orders that the child should stay with them.

The Arrangements to Look After Children (S) Regulations 1996 apply to children in foster care. In particular, they require that siblings should be kept together, if possible and that the foster carers must agree to bring the child up in his or her own religion.
(For further detail on these Regulations, please refer to Part 4).

3.72 Private fostering (The Fostering of Children (S) Act 1984)

Private fostering arises where a parent arranges for a non-relative to care for a child for more than 28 days. The local authority must be notified of such an arrangement in order that it may check the suitability of the arrangements and thereafter make regular visits to the home. The local authority may take action to prevent private fostering, if it thinks that it is not in the best interests of the child.

A child in private foster care is **not** a looked after child (see Part 4).

3.8   Surrogacy

Section 27 (1) of The Human Fertilisation and Embryology Act 1990 states that the woman who carries the child will always be treated as the mother, irrespective of genetic ties.

This then raises the issue of how the commissioning "parents" acquire legal status. **Section 30 of the Act** provides the process whereby they must apply to the court within 6 months of the child's birth for a Parental Order. This is like adoption, but without the complicated processes and procedures. The effect of the order is that the commissioning "parents" will be treated as the legal parents of the child. Before granting the order the court must be satisfied that

- The commissioning "parents" are both over 18 and are married;
- The child is living with them;
- The surrogate mother agrees to the parental agreement;
- Her husband or partner also agrees, if he is presumed to be the father (see below);
- No money has changed hands other than for reasonable expenses.

Where a woman conceives through donated sperm, Section 28 (2) states that her husband or unmarried partner will be treated as the father of the child, if he consented to the treatment. An unmarried partner would not have automatic parental rights. The sperm donor is never treated as the father of the child.

Part Four
Child Care & Child Protection

Introduction

4.10   Child Protection Register

Appendix to Part Four - Resources for child witness

Part Four

Child Care & Child Protection

Introduction

The Human Rights Act 1998 and the UN Convention on the Rights of the Child apply to the law relating to children and young people and may affect the way the law is implemented. However, the UNCRC is not part of national law and cannot be enforced by the courts in the same way as the Human Rights Act. Please refer to Part Seven for a full explanation.

In addition, the Scottish Executive has published the Children's Charter (http://www.scotland.gov.uk/library5/education/pcypfs-13.asp)
and a Framework for Standards for Child Protection (http://www.scotland.gov.uk/library5/education/pcypfs-13.asp) giving guidance on how children who may be at risk of harm or abuse can expect to be protected.

In early 2003 the Scottish Parliament passed the Commissioner for Children and Young People (Scotland) Act 2003. This Act creates an independent Commissioner to champion the right s of children and young people. The general function of the Commissioner is to promote and safeguard the rights of children and young people. This includes everyone in Scotland up to the age of 18, and those up to 21 years who have been "looked after" by a local authority. In doing so, the Commissioner will have regard to the United Nations Convention on the Rights of the Child (UNCROC).

There are a number of principles which underpin the Act. These are that:
- the Commissioner is independent;
- the best interests of children and young people should be a primary consideration in all matters affecting them; *and*
- the views of children and young people should be taken into account in accordance with age and maturity.

In exercising the general function of promoting and safeguarding the rights of children and young people under the Act, the Commissioner must:

- promote an awareness of those rights amongst children, young people and adults;
- keep under review current law, policy and practice relating to those rights;
- promote best practice by service providers in relation to children and young people;
- promote, commission, and publish research;
- undertake investigations; *and*
- report to the Parliament.

The Commissioner can also conduct investigations into how service providers take rights, interests and views into account in decisions or actions affecting children and young people. The Commissioner cannot, however, undertake an investigation which only concerns an individual child or young person. In an investigation, the Commissioner has the power to call witnesses to attend and require the production of documents. It is anticipated that investigations will be rare. The current Commissioner is Kathleen Marshall. The web address is http://www.cypcommissioner.org.

4.0 The Protection of Children (S) Act 2003

The Protection of Children (Scotland) Act 2003 allows Scottish Ministers to maintain a list of persons deemed unsuitable to work with children. The list is known as the Disqualified from Working with Children List and it covers both employed persons and volunteers of all categories and occupations.

'Child' means a person under the age of 18 years.

The List and Disclosure
The list not only provides organisations with the names of persons who are disqualified from working with children because they have committed an offence against children but also provides information on persons who have been referred to Ministers and subsequently placed on the list because of the evidence supplied in the referral.

Access to this list is only available through the Disclosure process, thereby making registration for police checks on new staff and volunteers mandatory. Also, existing staff and volunteers – even if they have already been the subject of disclosure checks - have to be checked again.

Offences by Organisations

All organisations that work with children, including voluntary organisations,commit an offence and are liable for prosecution if they do not comply with this legislation. They have a duty to make a referral to Scottish Ministers when any person (paid or unpaid):

- harms a child or puts a child at risk of harm, *and*
- is dismissed or is moved away from children as a consequence.

All organisations also have a duty to make a referral to Scottish Ministers when any person (paid or unpaid):

- harms a child or puts a child at risk of harm, *and*
- would have been dismissed if s/he had not resigned or retired or been made redundant or left at the end of a temporary contract.

It is an offence if an organisation knowingly

- employs a person to a position working with children *or*
- procures work for a person to a position working with children *or*
- fails to remove a person from a position working with children if that person is named on the List.

Offences by Listed Individuals

Individuals who are 'fully listed' (i.e. confirmed onto the list) commit a criminal offence if they apply to work or work with children. They will know if they are included on the list because they will be informed. If a person who is listed applies for a position to work with children, Disclosure Scotland or the Criminal Records Bureau (CRB) will notify the appropriate authorities that a named person has made application to work with children.

It is not an offence for an individual to apply to work or work with children if only 'provisionally listed' (i.e. been referred to Ministers but not (or not yet) confirmed onto the list). However, disclosure checks will reveal that such an individual is 'provisionally listed'.

Note that as at February 2008, there is no equivalent legislation in force covering people working with vulnerable adults, but the Protection of Vulnerable Groups (Scotland) Act 2007 will introduce measures to set up a list of persons unsuitable to work with vulnerable adults.

4.1 Children's Hearings

The Children (S) Act 1995
The Children's Hearings (S) Rules 1996

The Children's Hearing or Panel deals with children who are in need of care and protection, either because they are offending or because they are at risk in some other way.

The Reporter to the Children's Panel decides whether a child needs to be referred to the Panel which consists of 3 lay members.

There is no lower age limit for referring a child to the Panel and a child may be referred up to the age of **16** or **18**, if the child is already on supervision.

The overarching principles apply to proceedings relating to the Panel

- the welfare of the child throughout childhood is paramount;
- the child must be given an opportunity to express a view and that view must be taken into account. (The child may express a view in writing or in person to the Panel members);
- no order must be made unless it benefits the child.

4.10 Who has a right to attend the Panel?

- the child;
- relevant persons, i.e any person with parental responsibilities and rights and any person who has charge or control over the child, except in the course of employment;
- the press;

- each relevant person and each child has the right to take a representative to the Hearing for support. This representative may be anyone of their choice, but if they wish to take a legal representative, there is no legal aid available for legal representation at the Hearing.

In the case of S v Miller (2001 SLT 531) (www.scotcourts.gov.uk) the Court of Session looked at various aspects of the children's hearing system in relation to human rights. The court concluded that the hearing is an independent and impartial tribunal in accordance with Article 6, but the fact that legal aid is not available for legal representation has now been addressed as it would have been a breach of Article 6. The children's hearing system now has a process whereby legal representation can be made available for a child. However, the child cannot demand representation, since the Panel decides whether it is appropriate for him or her to have it. The child also has no choice about who the representative will be, since they are taken from an approved list.

Professionals do not have an automatic right to attend the Panel. They will be invited to attend and may be asked to leave after they have presented their information to the Panel.

4.11   Who may be legally excluded from the Panel?
- the press;
- a relevant person;

4.12   Who may refer a child to the Reporter?
Any person, but local authority employees may have a duty to refer the child, if the child appears to need compulsory measures of supervision. **Section 53 of the Children (S) Act 1995** places a legal duty on the local authority to refer a child to the Reporter **if it appears that the child may need compulsory measures of supervision.** Note that there is no requirement to show a risk of significant harm nor is it required to find a ground for referral. It is the job of the Reporter to establish a ground for referral.

Health professionals will normally be asked to make referrals through the social work department under child protection procedures. However, there is nothing in law to prevent a health professional from referring direct to the Reporter.

4.13 How does the Reporter decide whether to refer a child to the Panel?

The Reporter must be satisfied that at least one of the following grounds for referral exist and that the child is also in need of compulsory supervision.

The grounds for referral are:

- the child is outwith the control of any relevant person;
- the child is falling into bad associations or is exposed to moral danger;
- the child is suffering from lack of parental care;
- a Schedule One offence (see below) had been committed against the child;
- the child is or is likely to become part of a household where there is a child against whom a Schedule One offence has been committed;
- the child is or is likely to become part of a household where there is a person who has committed a Schedule One offence;
- the child has failed to attend school regularly without reasonable excuse;
- the child has committed an offence (the age of criminal responsibility is 8);
- the child has misused drugs or alcohol;
- the child has misused a volatile substance;
- the child is already "looked after" by the local authority and needs to be subject to compulsory supervision;
- the sheriff has made an antisocial behaviour order and requires the Reporter to refer the child (not already on supervision) to a children's hearing.

4.14 What are Schedule One offences?

Offences against a person under **17** years including sexual offences, other offences involving bodily injury and offences involving neglect or ill-treatment. **(Schedule One of The Criminal Procedure (S) Act 1995).**

If the Reporter thinks that a Hearing is not necessary, he or she may refer the child for voluntary social work help. **This does not prevent the child being referred to the Reporter again at a later date.**

4.15 What rights do relevant persons and the child have?

- the right to attend the Hearing;
- the right to take a representative;
- the right to see all papers which the Panel members see (the child does not have this right);
- the right to accept or reject the grounds of referral at the start of the Hearing;
- the right to appeal to the Sheriff against any decision of the Panel within 21 days of that decision;
- the right to call a review Hearing 3 months after the supervision requirement was made or last reviewed.

4.16 The process

At the start of the Hearing, the chairperson must explain the grounds of referral to each relevant person and each child. If any of them does not or cannot accept the grounds, the Panel may either discharge the case or refer it to the Sheriff for the Reporter to prove that the grounds of referral exist. If the Sheriff finds the grounds established, the case is referred back to the Panel for a decision about whether compulsory measures of supervision are required. The Panel may either discharge the case or make a supervision requirement.

4.17 Supervision requirement

This may require the child to live at home under supervision from the social work department or to live away from home either with foster carers or in a residential setting.

The Panel may attach any condition it thinks appropriate to the supervision requirement, including a condition restricting or terminating contact. It may also require unmet health needs to be addressed and may require the child to have assessment and/or treatment. However, the Panel cannot override a child's competent refusal of medical treatment.

The Panel cannot impose conditions on parents, but they can ask the Reporter to apply to the Sheriff for a Parenting Order. This is a civil order which requires parents to attend parenting classes for up to 3 months and makes the parents accountable for the child's behaviour. Breach of the order is a criminal offence.

The local authority has a duty to carry out the terms of the supervision requirement and if it is unable to do so or if there needs to be change, they must ask for a review hearing. The local authority may ask for a review at any time, but must ask for one if it intends to apply for freeing for adoption (see Part 3) or a Parental Responsibilities Order (see below). If the local authority fails to comply with the terms of a supervision requirement, the Reporter may ask the sheriff to order it to do so.

The supervision requirement may last for up to a year, but must be reviewed, if it is to last longer. A child may remain on supervision until age 18, but must not be kept on supervision longer than necessary.

A supervision requirement does **not** transfer parental responsibilities and rights to the local authority.

4.18   What happens if the Panel is unable to make a decision?

If , for example, the case is referred to the Sheriff for proof, the Panel may feel that the child should not return home in the meantime. The Panel has authority to make a **place of safety warrant** which keeps the child in a place of safety for 22 days. This may be renewed by the Panel for 2 further periods of 22 days each.

A child subject to a place of safety warrant or a supervision requirement is a **looked after child** (see below).

4.19   Changes Introduced by the Antisocial Behaviour etc (S) Act 2004

The **Antisocial Behaviour etc (Scotland) Act 2004** makes three new provisions in relation to children's hearings.

Section 135 introduces a new power for children's hearings to impose conditions restricting movement if a young person meets the criteria for secure accommodation as set out under S. 70 (10) of the Children (Scotland) Act 1995. If a young person meets the secure criteria, children's hearings will then consider whether a secure authorisation or a condition restricting movement is the most appropriate disposal.

Section 136 clarifies that local authorities have a statutory duty to implement decisions of children's hearings contained in supervision requirements. It also empowers hearings to require the Reporter to apply for an Order from the sheriff court requiring a local authority in breach of its duty to perform that duty.

Section 137 gives the Reporter and a children's hearing power to refer the case of a child who has been excluded from school to Scottish Ministers if it appears that the local authority concerned has failed to comply with its duty under section 14(3) of the Education (Scotland) Act 1980 to provide education to a pupil excluded from school.

4.2 Child Protection Order (Sections 57-60 The Children (S) Act 1995)

This is an emergency order.
Any person may apply to the Sheriff for this order which may require the child to be removed from home or to be kept where they are. Most applications come from a local authority.

The grounds for this order are:-

- that there are reasonable grounds to believe that a child is being treated or neglected so as to suffer significant harm or will suffer such harm if not removed to and kept in a place of safety, or kept safely where he or she is *and*
- the order is necessary to protect the child.

The local authority may also apply if:-

- it has reasonable grounds to suspect that the child is being or will be treated or neglected so as to suffer significant harm *and*
- it is making enquiries to investigate *and*
- these enquiries are being frustrated because access to the child is being unreasonably denied.

If a CPO is granted by the Sheriff the child must come before the Panel on the 2nd working day after it is used, so that the Panel may either continue the order or decide that it is not required. The Panel may also change any conditions in the order. If the order is continued, the child must come before the Panel again on the 8th working day after the order was used. This will be a full hearing as described above.

A CPO must be used within 24 hours of being granted.

It does **not** transfer parental responsibilities and rights to the local authority.

A child subject to a CPO is a **looked after child** (see below).

4.3   Child Assessment Order (Section 55 The Children (S) Act 1995)

Only a local authority may apply for a Child Assessment Order. The grounds for the order are as follows:-

- there is reasonable cause to suspect that the child is being treated or neglected so as to be suffering or likely to suffer significant harm *and*
- an assessment is necessary in order to establish whether there has been such treatment of the child *and*
- the assessment will not be carried out unless the order is granted.

The order lasts for a maximum of 7 days and can authorise removal of the child.

The order gives authority for assessment of the child irrespective of parental consent, but it **cannot** override a competent refusal by the child.

4.4 Exclusion Order (Sections 76-80 The Children (S) Act 1995)

Only the local authority may apply for this order and the grounds are as follows:

* the child has suffered, is suffering or is likely to suffer significant harm due to the conduct of a named person *and*
* the order is necessary to protect the child from the named person and is a better safeguard than removing the child from home *and*
* there will be an appropriate person left behind in the family home to care for the child and any other dependants.

The order can last for a maximum of 6 months and may be used to exclude someone from the home even if that person does not live there permanently.

An excluded person does **not** lose parental responsibilities and rights, if they had them.

A child subject to an Exclusion Order is a **looked after child** (see below).

4.5 Parental Responsibilities Order (Sections 86-89 The Children (S) Act 1995)

If the local authority needs to remove parental responsibilities and rights from a parent, it must apply to the Sheriff for a PRO on one or more of the following grounds:-

* the parent consents to responsibilities and rights being removed;
* the parent is not known, cannot be found or is incapable of giving agreement;
* the parent is withholding consent unreasonably;
* the parent has failed without reasonable cause to fulfil parental responsibilities and rights;
* the parent has seriously ill-treated the child whose reintegration into the household is unlikely.

These grounds are the same as the grounds for dispensing with consent to adoption or freeing for adoption.

A PRO is often used as a first step towards adoption and it transfers all parental responsibilities and rights to the local authority, **except** the right to consent to adoption and freeing for adoption.

A child who is subject to a PRO is a **looked after child** and has a stated right to maintain contact with persons whose parental responsibilities and rights have been removed.

When it comes into force, the **Adoption and Children (Scotland) Act 2007** will make provision for a Permanence Order which will replace a Parental Responsibilities Order.

4.6   The Duty To Accommodate a Child (Section 25 The Children (S) Act 1995)

The local authority has a duty to provide accommodation for a child under the age of 18 if any of the following grounds exist:-

- if no one has parental responsibilities for the child;
- if the child is lost or abandoned;
- if the person who has been caring for the child is prevented from doing so, either permanently or temporarily.

This is not a compulsory form of care like a supervision requirement or a court order. A child under 16 may not be accommodated, if a person with parental responsibilities and rights objects and is willing and able to care for the child.

A child may be accommodated with a foster carer or in a residential setting.

An accommodated child is a **looked after child.** Accommodating a child has **no** effect on parental responsibilities and rights, unless the child has been accommodated for more than 6 months, in which case, parents must give 14 days notice of their intention to remove the child.

4.7 Looked After Child (Section 17 The Children (S) Act 1995)

The following children are looked after:-

- A child on supervision from the Panel **(Section 70 of The Children (S) Act 1995);**
- A child under a child protection order, child assessment order or exclusion order;
- A child who is accommodated **(Section 25 of The Children (S) Act 1995);**
- A child who is subject to a Parental Responsibilities and Rights Order **(Section 86 of The Children (S) Act 1995);**
- A child who has transferred to Scotland under an order made in other parts of the UK.

The local authority has the following duties to a looked after child:-

- to safeguard and promote the welfare of the child which is paramount;
- to make use of services to keep the child at home, where appropriate;
- to promote regular direct contact between the child and a person with parental responsibilities and rights;
- to prepare the child for ceasing to be looked after;
- to take into account the views of the child and other relevant persons before making any decisions about the child;
- to take into account the child's religious, cultural, racial and linguistic background;
- to draw up and maintain a care plan for the child;
- to review the child's case regularly.

The Arrangements to Look After Children (S) Regulations set out the timings for reviews:-

- for a child looked after at home within 3 months of becoming looked after and then at least every 6 months;

- for a child looked after away from home within 6 weeks of the placement and then within 3 months and then at least every 6 months.

In addition, under **Section 29** the local authority has a duty to give leaving care support to any young person under 19 who was looked after at age 16 or later and is no longer looked after.

The Regulation of Care (Scotland) Act 2001 increased local authority duties to looked after children as follows:
Section 73 (1) amends section 29 of The Children (S) Act 1995 to include duties on local authorities to:

- Carry out an assessment of the needs of young people who have been looked after who they have a duty or power to advise, guide or assist under section 29;
- Establish a procedure for considering representations, including complaints, made to them about the discharge of their functions under section 29.

New Regulations and guidance were issued by the Scottish Executive in April 2004 in order to help local authorities to fulfil all of their duties to looked after children. The guidance can be found at http://www.scotland.gov.uk/library5/education/syplc-01.asp

The guidance makes it clear that local authorities must seek and take account of the views and wishes of the young person in assessing their needs and in preparing the plan that comes out of the assessment. If there are meetings, the authority should take steps to make sure that the young person can attend and take part, for example by paying travel and subsistence costs or providing an interpreter. The young person has a right to receive copies of relevant documents and the right to refuse consent for the sharing of information.

The guidance also emphasises there is now a statutory duty for local authorities to carry out an assessment of the needs of **all** young people over school age leaving their care. This includes young people looked after at home, not just those provided with accommodation by the authority.

4.8 Child in Need (Sections 22-24 of The Children (S) Act 1995)

A child is in need if:-

- s/he is unlikely to achieve or maintain a reasonable standard of health or development, unless services are provided;
- his/her health or development is likely to be significantly impaired or further impaired, unless services are provided;
- s/he is disabled;
- s/he is affected adversely by the disability of another family member.

The local authority has a duty to promote and safeguard the welfare of such children. Services may be provided to the child or to other family members, if that is in the best interests of the child.

If the child is disabled or affected by disability, the local authority has a duty, **if requested to do so,** to carry out an assessment of the needs of that child and any other disabled person in the family. It must also assess the ability of a carer to provide care for the disabled child.

The local authority has a duty to provide day care for a child under 5 who is in need and a duty to provide after school and holiday care for a child in need who attends school.

4.9 Childminding and Day Care (The Regulation of Care (S) Act 2001)

A childminder is someone who:-

- looks after one or more children under 16 in a private house for payment for more than 2 hours in any day and is not a parent, relative or foster carer and does not have parental responsibilities and rights for the child or children.

Childminders must register with the Care Commission. Failure to do so is a criminal offence.

People who provide day care for children under 16 for more than 2 hours per day must also register with the Care Commission.

4.10   Child Protection Register

This part has dealt with the legal provisions in the Children (S) Act 1995. However, even before these provisions come into play, guidance on child protection provides a mechanism for dealing with concerns at a very early stage.

The local authority must maintain a Child Protection Register of all children who are subject to an inter-agency child protection plan. This alerts agencies to the fact that there are professional concerns about a child and requires the inter-agency plan to be reviewed every six months. The decision to place a child on the Register is taken at a Child Protection Case Conference which is a multi-agency case conference attended by those professionals who are involved with the child and the family. The child and the family should be empowered to participate fully in the proceedings and should be allowed to take someone with them for support. The child and the family are likely to need support to understand the process in which they are involved and to overcome their anxieties.

The categories of abuse under which the child may be registered are:
* Physical abuse;
* Sexual abuse;
* Non-organic failure to thrive;
* Emotional abuse;
* Physical neglect.

A child should be placed on the Register when:
* One or more of the above criteria are met *and*
* The child's safety and welfare requires an inter-agency child protection plan.

The Child Protection Case Conference also decides when to remove a child from the Register and the arrangements for an inter-agency plan.

The Child Protection Register and Child Protection Case Conferences are dealt with under Guidance, not legislation. The document 'Child Protection – A Shared Responsibility' (Scottish Office, 1998c) contains full details of practice

and procedure in this area. New Guidance on Child Protection Committees was issued in January 2005 by the Scottish Executive at
http://www.scotland.gov.uk/library5/education/pcypcpc-00.asp

A child does not have to be on the Register before legal intervention under the Children (S) Act 1995 may take place. Equally, a child on the Register will not always be subject to legal intervention under the Children (S) Act 1995.

Note: that being on the Register does not give the child any real legal protection. It is simply a mechanism for alerting professionals to concerns about the child.

Part Four - Appendix 1
Resources for Child
Witnesses

The Scottish Executive has produced the following publications:

http://www.scotland.gov.uk/Publications/2005/07/07105526/55283
Being a Witness for Children in Criminal Proceedings

http://www.scotland.gov.uk/Publications/2005/06/28154343/43454
Being a Witness for Young People in Criminal Proceedings

http://www.scotland.gov.uk/Publications/2005/06/2984605/46120
Being a Witness for Children in Children's Hearing Proceedings

http://www.scotland.gov.uk/Publications/2005/06/28141320/13224
Being a Witness for Young People in Children's Hearing Proceedings

http://www.scotland.gov.uk/Publications/2005/06/27110833/08419
Your Child is a Witness – A Booklet for Parents and Carers

http://www.scotland.gov.uk/Publications/2007/11/22120443/0
A Guide to the Vulnerable Witnesses (Scotland) Act 2004

Part Five
Mental Health &
Community Care

5.3 Community Care Legislation

5.4 Adult Protection

Part Five

Mental Health & Community Care

5.1 The Mental Health (Care and Treatment) (S) Act 2003

The Mental Health (Care and Treatment) (Scotland) Act 2003 came into force in October 2005. It **replaces** the Mental Health (Scotland) Act 1984. The Act does not focus on detention in hospital, rather it expects that compulsion in the community will be considered first. The Act does not focus only on compulsion. It also covers the provision of services.

5.10 Key definitions and principles:-

The 2003 Act has a set of principles in section1 that apply to anyone exercising functions under the Act. The principles state that regard must be had to the following:

- The present and past wishes and feelings of the patient
- The views of -

    The patient's named person;
    Any carer of the patient;
    Any guardian of the patient; *and*
    Any welfare attorney of the patient.
- The importance of the patient participating as fully as possible;
- The importance of providing such information and support to the patient as is necessary to enable the patient to participate;
- The range of options available in the patient's case;
- The importance of providing the maximum benefit to the patient;
- The need to ensure that, unless it can be shown that it is justified in the circumstances, the patient is not treated in a way that is less favourable than the way in which a person who is not a patient might be treated in a comparable situation;

- The patient's abilities, background and characteristics, including, without prejudice to that generality, the patient's age, sex, sexual orientation, religious persuasion, racial origin, cultural and linguistic background and membership of any ethnic group.

The principle of minimum intervention also applies.

The welfare of a patient who is a child is paramount.

Mental Disorder means mental illness, personality disorder and learning disability A person is not mentally disordered by reason only of sexual orientation, sexual deviancy, trans-sexualism, transvestism, dependence on, or use of, alcohol or drugs, behaviour that causes, or is likely to cause, harassment, alarm or distress to any other person, or by acting as no prudent person would act.

Mental Health Officer (MHO) means a social worker with specialist training in mental health. The MHO must be involved in the following:

- the granting of a short-term detention certificate;
- the making of an interim compulsory treatment order;
- the making of a compulsory treatment order;
- the making of an assessment order;
- the making of a treatment order;
- the making of an interim compulsion order;
- the making of a compulsion order;
- the making of a hospital direction;
- the making of a transfer for treatment direction.

Duties of MHO
- To produce a Social Circumstances Report;
- To apply for a CTO, if s/he receives 2 medical reports certifying that the grounds exist;
- To produce a care plan to accompany the application for a CTO;
- To inform relevant parties of the application and in the case of the patient and the named person, of their right to object to the application and of their legal rights;
- To assist the patient in the process of nominating a named person;
- To identify whether a named person has been appointed;

- To explain the right to independent advocacy and assist the patient to access advocacy services and/or legal representation;
- To consult on the existence or creation of advanced statements;
- To refer to the local authority for a comprehensive community care assessment when required and when the MHO himself or herself is not completing one.

Powers of MHO

A Mental Health Officer may:
- apply for a warrant from the sheriff to enter premises where there is a duty to enquire about the welfare of a person with a mental disorder, but entry cannot be gained(s.35);
- apply for a warrant to remove the person to a place of safety [s.293].

The Mental Welfare Commission (MWC) is based in Edinburgh and can investigate complaints and authorise discharge of a patient. It must be notified of all patients under compulsion.

The Responsible Medical Officer (RMO) means the doctor responsible for the treatment of the patient.

Approved Medical Practitioner (AMP) specialist doctor

Designated Medical Practitioner (DMP) a doctor designated by the Mental Welfare Commission to deal with issues that require a second opinion

Named Person means a person appointed by the patient to be involved in their case. Under the 1984 Act, a patient's nearest relative **was** a key person who would have been involved in discussions about treatment and would have had access to confidential information about the patient Under the 2003 Act, a person aged 16 and over with a mental disorder has the right to nominate at any time, in writing, **a named person of their choice to take on the role that would have previously been held by the nearest relative.** The named person does not have to be a relative. If it is not possible to nominate a named person or if the person declines to act, the primary carer would be the named person. If the primary carer is not available, only then does the nearest relative act. The patient must have the capacity to understand the decision they are making and its effects. To be valid, a nomination must be signed by the person making it and witnessed by a prescribed person. The prescribed person must certify that the person signing the nomination understands its effect and has not been subject to any undue influence. The named person has similar rights to the patient including the right to:

- Apply to the Tribunal;
- Appear and be represented at the Tribunal in relation to a CTO;
- Appeal against short term compulsion;
- Have access to information when the patient is under compulsion or when compulsion is planned.

Information about appointing a named person can be found at
http://www.scotland.gov.uk/library5/health/mhgnp-00.asp

Advance Statement
The 2003 Act gives recognition to advance statements about treatment for a mental disorder. The statement must be in writing and must be witnessed. When a person comes under compulsion, a doctor treating that person must have regard to the advance statement and if the doctor decides to treat the patient against the wishes expressed in the statement, that must be reported to the Mental Welfare Commission.

Information about making an advance statement can be found at
http://www.scotland.gov.uk/library5/health/mhgas-00.asp

Mental Health Tribunal will hear applications for a Compulsory Treatment Order and appeals.

Treatment under the Act covers:
- (a) nursing;
- (b) care;
- (c) psychological intervention;
- (d) habilitation (including education, and training in work, social and independent living skills); *and*
- (e) rehabilitation.

Unlawful Detention
The Act creates a new right of appeal to the Tribunal against unlawful detention. This would cover the situation where a patient had been admitted voluntarily, but now wishes to leave and feels that he or she is being kept in hospital under threat of detention.

Local Authority Duties

The 2003 Act places duties on local authorities to provide care and support services and to promote the well-being and social development of all persons in their area who have, or have had, a mental disorder; also to carry out a community care assessment and to investigate cases where there is concern about the welfare of a person. The new duties to provide care and support services (as defined in the Regulation of Care (Scotland) Act 2001) replace the rather vague duty to provide after care services under section 8 of the 1984 Act.

Right to Independent Advocacy

The Act also creates a right to independent advocacy for any person with a mental disorder. There is a duty on either the MHO or hospital managers to advise the person about this right. Guidance states that the information must be given in accessible format and that the mere handing over of a leaflet will be insufficient. If the patient wishes to have an independent advocate, there is a duty to assist the person to access an advocacy service.

The following provisions apply to persons who are NOT involved in the criminal law system.

5.11 Emergency Detention

requires the certification of one doctor (may be the GP) of the following grounds

- the patient has a mental disorder;
- because of that mental disorder, the patient's decision-making ability with regard to medical treatment for that mental disorder is significantly impaired;
- it is necessary as a matter of urgency to detain the patient in hospital in order to determine what medical treatment should be provided to the patient for the suspected mental disorder;
- there would be a significant risk to the health, safety or welfare of the patient or to the safety of another person if the patient were not detained in hospital;
- making arrangements with a view to granting a short-term detention certificate would involve undesirable delay.

Consent

The doctor must obtain the consent of a Mental Health Officer, unless it is not practicable to do so. This form of detention may be used for a person in the community or a voluntary patient in hospital. In the case of a voluntary patient in hospital, a psychiatric nurse may detain the patient for up to two hours, in order to give time for a doctor to be found. If the doctor arrives after the first hour, the period of detention may be extended for a further hour from the time of arrival, in order to give time for assessment.

Period of detention

Up to 72 hours

Treatment

The Act gives no authority for treatment without consent in this 72-hour period, but doctors may use a common law power to treat if, for example, the patient needs to be sedated.

Emergency detention may be used for a person in the community or a voluntary patient who wishes to leave hospital.

A nurse may detain a voluntary patient for up to 2 hours in hospital whilst a doctor is found to authorise emergency detention. If the doctor arrives in the second hour, the period may be extended for up to an hour from when s/he arrives.

Under the 2003 Act emergency detention is only to be used in EXCEPTIONAL circumstances. The preferred method for bringing a patient under compulsion is short term detention.

5.12   Short Term Detention

Grounds

An Approved Medical Practitioner (AMP) must certify that:

- the patient has a mental disorder;
- because of the mental disorder, the patient's ability to make decisions about the provision of medical treatment is significantly impaired;

- that it is necessary to detain the patient in hospital for the purpose of determining what medical treatment should be given to the patient; or giving medical treatment to the patient;
- that if the patient were not detained in hospital there would be a significant risk to the health, safety or welfare of the patient; or to the safety of any other person; *and*
- that the granting of a short-term detention certificate is necessary.

The AMP must obtain the consent of a Mental Health Officer (MHO).

Period of detention

The patient may be detained for up to **28** days.
If the patient deteriorates near the end of the 28-day period and there is insufficient time to lodge an application with the Tribunal, the patient may be detained for a further three working days if the AMP issues an extension certificate certifying:

- that the patient has a mental disorder;
- that, because of the mental disorder, the patient's ability to make decisions about the medical treatment to be provided for that mental disorder is significantly impaired;
- that it is necessary to detain the patient in hospital for the purpose of determining what medical treatment should be given or of giving medical treatment to the patient;
- that there would be a significant risk to the health, safety or welfare of the patient or to the safety of another person if the patient were not detained in hospital;
- that because of a change in the mental health of the patient, an application for a Compulsory Treatment Order should be made.

Appeal

The patient or named person has one right of appeal to the Tribunal in the 28-day period.

Treatment

The patient may be treated without consent for his or her mental disorder, subject to those treatments requiring special consent.

5.13 Compulsory Treatment Order (may authorise compulsory treatment in the community or in hospital)

Grounds
- the patient has a mental disorder;
- medical treatment which would be likely to prevent the mental disorder worsening; or alleviate any of the symptoms, or effects, of the disorder, is available for the patient;
- if the patient were not provided with such medical treatment there would be a significant risk to the health, safety or welfare of the patient; or to the safety of any other person;
- because of the mental disorder the patient's ability to make decisions about the provision of such medical treatment is significantly impaired; *and*
- the making of a compulsory treatment order is necessary.

This must be certified by two doctors – an Approved Medical Practitioner (AMP) and the patient's GP or two AMP's– who must agree on at least one form of mental disorder. There must be no more than five days between the two doctors having seen the patient

Who may apply?
A Mental Health Officer must apply for a CTO if s/he receives 2 medical reports certifying that the grounds exist. The application must be made within 14 days of the last medical examination.

An application for a CTO consists of:
- two mental health reports prepared by the medical practitioners;
- the mental health officer's report prepared under section 61 of the Act;
- the proposed care plan produced by the MHO under section 62 of the Act.

It must specify:
- the compulsory measures that are being sought in relation to the patient (i.e. which of the compulsory measures listed at section 66(1) of the Act are being sought);

- the medical treatment, community care services, relevant services and any other forms of treatment, care or service which it is proposed will be provided to the patient;
- the name of the hospital whose managers will appoint the patient's RMO. (This is only required where the proposed CTO seeks to impose community-based requirements.)

Period of detention or compulsion

The Tribunal places the patient under compulsion initially for six months .

Renewal of CTO

The Responsible Medical Officer renews detention by lodging a report with the Tribunal. The Tribunal **may** review the RMO's decision, but **must** review it if the RMO applies to extend the CTO **and** vary the conditions in it. The CTO can be renewed for 6 months and then for 12 months at a time thereafter.

Appeal

The patient or the named person have a right to apply to the tribunal (section 99 and 100). There are two types of applications which the patient or the patient's named person can make to the Tribunal. They are:

- an application under section 99 of the Act to revoke a determination to extend a CTO;
- an application under section 100 of the Act to revoke a CTO or to vary any of the compulsory measures or recorded matters specified in the CTO.

With regard to the application to revoke an RMO's section 86 determination to extend a CTO, such an application can be made at any point during the CTO's operation after the point where the RMO has made that section 86 determination.

With regard to the application to revoke or vary the CTO, such an application cannot be made within three months of:

- the CTO being made;
- an order which extends the CTO following a section 86 determination;
- an order which extends the CTO and varies the compulsory measures and/or recorded matters specified in the CTO.

If the Tribunal refuses the application, there are restrictions on the number of further applications which can be made to the Tribunal. Section 100 states that the person who made the application (i.e. the patient or the named person) may not make the same application again within each 6 month or 12 month period of the CTO being in effect.

5.14 How may a patient be discharged?

- By the Mental Health Tribunal, if there is a right of appeal;
- By The Mental Welfare Commission;
- By the RMO if any of the grounds for compulsion cease to exist.

5.15 Treatment for the mental disorder

Under the 2003 Act ECT will **not** be permitted if the patient is competent to refuse. Under the 1984 Act, ECT could be given to a patient who was competent to refuse, if a second doctor authorised it. Drug treatment that will last more than 2 months also requires special safeguards involving a second doctor.

A person detained under the Mental Health (Care and Treatment) (Scotland) Act 2003 does not necessarily lack the legal capacity to consent to or refuse medical treatment. However, a patient under compulsion under one of the procedures listed below (other than in the 72-hour emergency period) may be treated for his or her mental disorder without his or her consent even if he or she makes or has made a competent refusal.

- a short-term detention certificate;
- a compulsory treatment order;
- an interim compulsory treatment order;
- an assessment order; (criminal law)
- a treatment order; (criminal Law)
- a compulsion order (with or without restrictions); (criminal law)
- an interim compulsion order; (criminal law)
- a hospital direction; (criminal law) *and*
- a transfer for treatment direction. (criminal law)

The following authorities to detain do **not** authorise treatment without consent, unless it is a genuine emergency:
- an emergency detention certificate;

- a nurse's power to detain pending a medical examination;
- the power to hold a person under the place of safety provisions or removal from a public place provisions;
- a place of safety warrant;
- a removal order.

Treatment for a physical condition is not covered by the Act. If a patient is unable to consent to physical treatment, doctors would need to establish whether the patient has a welfare attorney or welfare guardian appointed to him or her. If there is no one appointed with the authority to give medical consent, doctors must then decide whether to proceed without consent on the grounds of necessity under the Adults with Incapacity (Scotland) Act 2000 or whether to apply to court for permission to treat the patient. Doctors must ascertain whether the patient has previously made a competent advance statement refusing a specific type of treatment.

Some treatments for a mental disorder under the 2003 Act require special consents.

Treatment requiring consent AND a second opinion

Any surgical operation for destroying brain tissue or destroying the functioning of brain tissue requires the consent of the patient in writing and two lay persons appointed by the Mental Welfare Commission must certify that the patient is able to consent and has done so. In addition, a DMP must confirm both that the patient has consented and that the treatment is in the patient's best interests. The patient can withdraw consent to the treatment at any time.

For patients who are incapable of consenting, a designated medical practitioner must certify that this is the case, that the patient does not object to the treatment and that the treatment is in the patient's best interests. Two lay persons appointed by the Mental Welfare Commission must certify that the patient is incapable of consenting and that the patient does not object to the treatment. In addition, the responsible medical officer must apply to the Court of Session, and the Court must make an order authorising the treatment specified. The Court of Session may only authorise the treatment if satisfied that, having regard to the likelihood of the treatment alleviating or preventing a deterioration in the patient's condition, it is in the best interests of the patient, and the patient does not object.

Treatment requiring consent

Electroconvulsive therapy (ECT) requires the consent of the patient. A designated medical practitioner approved by the Mental Welfare Commission may only authorize ECT with the RMO if the patient is unable to consent.

Treatment requiring consent or a second opinion
Any drug treatment that lasts more than two months requires the agreement of a designated medical practitioner.

Advance Statements
If the patient has made an advance statement about treatment for his or her mental disorder, those treating the patient must have regard to this. If it is decided not to follow the advance statement, this must be reported to the MWC.

Any treatment which does not relate to the mental disorder requires normal consent.

Doctors use a three stage test to establish whether a person is able to consent:

- is the patient able to take in and retain the information?
- does the patient believe the information?
- is the patient able to make an informed choice?

5.16   Suspension of Conditions
Patients under compulsion may have conditions in their CTO suspended by the RMO. This replaces the concept of leave of absence.

5.17   Detention by the police
The police have the power to remove a person to a place of safety if that person is found in a public place apparently suffering from a mental disorder and in need of immediate care and treatment. The patient may be detained for up to 24 hours and his or her Nearest Relative and the local authority must be informed as soon as possible.

5.18   Warrant to enter premises and removal orders
The sheriff or a JP may issue a warrant authorising the MHO or the police to enter premises and may further grant a removal order in relation to a person aged 16 and over who has a mental disorder and is likely to suffer significant harm if not removed to a place of safety.

5.2   Legal capacity

This means having the ability to understand the meaning and consequence of decisions and being able to make a true choice.

A person of 16 or over must either make decisions for himself or herself or must have a person legally appointed to them. Parents may not continue to make decisions for a child who is 16 or over, unless legally appointed to do so. This means that parents or "next of kin" of a person aged 16 and over have no automatic right to access information about that person and may not sign legal forms on behalf of the person. The term "next of kin" has no legal meaning and is simply used as a means of identifying a person who can be contacted in an emergency.

Parents may act for a child under 16 because they still have parental rights.

5.20   The DWP Appointee

A person over the age of 18 may be appointed to act on behalf of someone in claiming, receiving and dealing with benefits, if the latter is unable to act for himself or herself. The person is appointed for an indefinite period and is personally responsible for any mistakes or overpayments. This appointment does not give any authority to deal with matters other than DWP benefits.

This appointment is not affected by The Adults With Incapacity (S) Act 2000 which sets out a range of appointments that may be made in relation to incapable adults.

5.21   The Power of Attorney

This is a document signed by a person whilst he or she still has legal capacity, giving another person or persons authority to act on his or her behalf. The powers given may be very specific or may be very wide and general. Powers of attorney often deal only with financial matters. The power of attorney is an excellent way of allowing a person who knows that they will lose legal capacity to make their own choice about who should act for them.

The Adults With Incapacity (S) Act 2000 makes special provision for powers of attorney intended to continue after loss of capacity.

5.22 Definition of incapable under The Adults With Incapacity (S) Act 2000

The definition of "incapable" is: incapable of acting or making decisions or communicating decisions or understanding decisions or retaining the memory of decisions in relation to any particular matter, by reason of mental disorder or of inability to communicate due to physical disability.

Incapacity must be assessed in relation to **each** decision, since an adult may have capacity to make some decisions, but may need help with more complex issues.

5.23 The overarching principles in The Adults With Incapacity (S) Act 2000

The Act contains the following overarching principles:

Principle 1 – Benefit
A person is not permitted to intervene in the life of the incapable adult unless satisfied that there is a benefit to the adult and that such benefit cannot be achieved without the intervention.

Principle 2 – Minimum Intervention
The intervention must be the least restrictive option in relation to the freedom of the incapable adult. For example, if a person has financial powers, but the adult is able to deal with small amounts of money himself or herself, the law requires that person to encourage the adult to use that ability, rather than taking complete control.

Principle 3 – Take Account of the Wishes of the Adult
The views of the incapable adult must be sought, by any means possible.

Principle 4 – Consultation With Relevant Others
The views of the nearest relative, the primary carer, any person already appointed to act for the adult and any other person who appears to be relevant must be sought.

Principle 5 – Encourage the Adult to Exercise Whatever Skills he or She Has
The adult must be encouraged to exercise whatever skills he or she has concerning property, financial affairs or personal welfare, and to develop new such skills.

5.24 List of appointments under The Adults With Incapacity (S) Act 2000

The list of possible appointments under the Act is:

- A continuing attorney appointed by an individual, while capable, to manage property and/or financial affairs. This may come into effect immediately and continue after incapacity or may come into effect upon incapacity.

- A welfare attorney appointed by an individual, while capable, to manage welfare matters after loss of capacity.

- A person authorized by The Public Guardian to use the funds of an incapable adult for the benefit of that adult.

- A guardian who may have financial and/or welfare powers and is appointed by the sheriff.

- A person authorized under an intervention order (welfare and/or financial) made by the sheriff to deal with a specific issue.

- The managers of authorized establishments, where there is no one else to manage an adult's finances, may be authorized to manage a resident's finances.

In addition, the Act makes provision for doctors to certify that an adult is incapable of consenting to medical treatment and to proceed to treat without consent, as long as the treatment is in the best interests of the patient. If the patient has a guardian or welfare attorney, that person should be consulted about the treatment. Certain treatments such as ECT and medication for mental disorder lasting more than 3 months are likely to be excluded from this authority to treat without consent.

Consent to medical treatment is covered in full in Part Six.

If you have any concerns about the personal welfare of an incapable adult, ask the local authority to investigate in accordance with its duties under the Act. If you are dissatisfied with the outcome of this investigation, you may ask the Mental Welfare Commission to investigate under the Act.

The Mental Welfare Commission
Argyle House
3 Lady Lawson Street
Edinburgh EH3 9SH
Tel: 0131 222 6111

www.mwcscot.org.uk

If you have concerns about the financial welfare of an incapable adult, you may ask the Public Guardian to investigate under the Act.

The Office of the Public Guardian
Callander Business Park
Falkirk FK1 1XR
Tel: 01324 678300

www.publicguardian-scotland.gov.uk

5.25 Continuing and Welfare Powers of Attorney under The Adults With Incapacity (S) Act 2000

The Act creates two new types of power of attorney. A power of attorney is a document signed by an individual when he or she has legal capacity, authorizing another person or persons to act on his or her behalf. This Act only applies to financial powers of attorney intended to continue after a person has lost legal capacity or powers of attorney relating to welfare matters (which can only come into effect after loss of legal capacity).

The general principles in Section 1 apply to continuing and welfare attorneys.

Continuing Powers of Attorney

A continuing power of attorney must:
- Be signed by the granter;
- Express a clear intention that it is intended to continue after loss of legal capacity;
- Incorporate a certificate from a solicitor or other prescribed person that the granter has been interviewed immediately prior to signing the document and that the granter understands the nature and content of the document and is not acting under undue influence;
- Be registered with The Public Guardian before it can come into effect;

- It may come into effect immediately upon registration or upon incapacity.

Welfare Powers of Attorney

A welfare power of attorney must:
- Be signed by the granter;
- Express a clear intention that it is intended to cover welfare matters;
- Incorporate a certificate from a solicitor or other prescribed person that the granter has been interviewed immediately prior to signing the document and that the granter understands the nature and content of the document and is not acting under undue influence;
- Be registered with The Public Guardian before it can come into effect;
- It cannot be used until the granter has lost legal capacity in relation to the matters covered by the power of attorney;
- It can only be given to an individual who may not be an officer of the local authority.

A welfare attorney may not:
- Place the granter in hospital for treatment of a mental disorder against his or her will;
- Give consent to any treatment covered by The Mental Health (Care and Treatment) (Scotland) Act 2003.

Continuing and welfare attorneys are required to keep records of the exercise of their powers. This does not apply to persons acting under powers of attorney made before April 2001. Powers of attorney made before April 2001 do not have to be registered.

5.26   Authority to Intromit With Funds

The Act makes a new provision whereby an individual may apply to The Public Guardian for authority to intromit (deal with) the funds of an incapable adult. This is a useful provision where a private individual is willing to act and is a good example of a fairly low level of intervention. It might be used to pay household bills on behalf of an adult who is incapable of managing that on his or her own.

The person who wishes to be appointed must complete a form available from The Public Guardian. The application must specify:
- The purpose for which the funds will be used;

- The names and addresses of the nearest relative and primary carer of the adult;
- The account from which money is to be transferred and an undertaking to open the designated account;
- The application must be accompanied by a medical certificate certifying incapacity;
- The Public Guardian must notify the adult, the nearest relative and the primary carer of the application and they may raise objections. The Public Guardian may refer to application to the sheriff for determination. There is a right of appeal against a decision to grant or refuse an application;
- If the application is granted, The Public Guardian will issue a certificate of authority stipulating that the withdrawer may open a designated account and how much money may be transferred from the adult's account to that designated account and at what intervals. The authority may be for up to 3 years;
- A designated account may not be overdrawn and the withdrawer must keep records of transactions on the account.

Provision will be made in 2008 for organisations to be permitted to apply for authority to intromit with funds.

A person authorized to intromit with funds is subject to the general principles in Section 1 of the Act.

5.27   Guardianship and Intervention Orders

Where there is a need for continuing intervention, a person claiming interest in the incapable adult may apply to the sheriff to be appointed as a guardian. Two medical reports certifying incapacity are required. In addition, for welfare guardianship, a report from a Mental Health Officer (mental disorder) or Chief Social Work Officer (all other cases) is required. For financial guardianship, a report from a person with sufficient knowledge of the appropriateness of the order and the suitability of the nominee is required. It is possible to appoint 2 or more persons as joint guardians or a guardian and a substitute. The court will consider the suitability of the nominated guardian and issues such as:

- Are they aware of the incapable adult's circumstances and needs?
- Are they aware of the role of a guardian and able to carry out their functions?

- Are they accessible to the incapable adult and the primary carer?
- Are there any conflicts of interest or undue concentrations of power?

A guardian will usually be appointed for 3 years, but other periods are possible. The guardian's powers will be strictly tailored to the needs of the incapable adult. This is the highest level of intervention.

Guardians with financial powers will be subject to supervision and scrutiny by the Public Guardian. Guardians with welfare powers will be subject to supervision by the local authority and subject to scrutiny by either the local authority or the Mental Welfare Commission.

The local authority has a duty to apply for guardianship where it appears necessary, but no one else applies.

A guardian is subject to the general principles in Section 1 of the Act.

Intervention Orders

Where there is a need for intervention, but not on a continuing basis, a person claiming interest may apply to the sheriff for an intervention order authorizing the particular intervention. These orders may cover welfare and/or financial matters. The reports required are the same as for guardianship orders. This type of short term intervention could be used, for example, where a property had to be sold, but the owner no longer had capacity to sign the documents.

A person acting under an intervention order is subject to the general principles in Section 1 of the Act.

5.28   Management of Residents' Funds By Managers of Residential Establishments

If there is no one to manage the funds of an incapable adult, the manager of a residential establishment may obtain a medical certificate certifying that the resident is incapable of managing his or her own funds. The manager then notifies the supervisory body that he or she intends to manage the resident's funds. The medical certificate must be renewed after 3 years. The manager is permitted to deal with the following matters:

- Claiming, receiving, holding and spending any pension, benefit or allowance or payment other than under The Social Security Contributions and Benefits Act 1992;
- Claiming, receiving, holding and spending any money to which the resident is entitled;
- Holding any other moveable property to which the resident is entitled and disposing of such property.

Managers have to keep records and **are subject to the general principles of the Act.**

5.3 Community Care Legislation

The Mental Health (Care and Treatment) (S) Act 2003 (in force October 2005)
The Community Care and Health (S) Act 2002
The Regulation of Care (S) Act 2001 and The National Care Standards
The National Health Service and Community Care Act 1990
The Social Work (S) Act 1968
The Disabled Persons (Services, Consultation and Representation) Act 1986
The Chronically Sick and Disabled Persons Act 1970
The National Assistance Act 1948
The Data Protection Act 1998
The Human Rights Act 1998

5.30 Community Care Services
These are defined as services for adults under

The Social Work (S) Act 1968 - includes a duty to provide domicilliary services and residential care to persons in need which is defined as:-

- persons who are suffering from illness or a mental disorder *or*
- persons who are substantially handicapped *or*
- persons who are drug or alcohol dependent;

- persons who have been released from prison or detention;
- persons in need of care and attention due to youth, age or infirmity.

The Mental Health Care and Treatment (S) Act 2003 - duties on local authorities to provide care and support services and to promote the well-being and social development of all persons in their area who have, or have had, a mental disorder

5.31 Assessment (Section 12A of The Social Work (S) Act 1968 inserted by the 1990 Act and amended by the 2002 Act).

The local authority has a duty to assess a person who appears to be in need of community care services. The local authority must then decide, based on

- the assessment *and*
- the amount of substantial and regular care provided by any carer *and*
- the views of both the client and the carer (consistent with Articles 6 and 10 of the European Convention on Human Rights)

whether the person requires the provision of services. This is known as a needs-led assessment. Whilst carrying out the assessment, if the person appears to be disabled (i.e. chronically sick or disabled or suffering from a mental disorder), the local authority has a **duty** to carry out a second assessment under **Section 4 of The Disabled Persons (Services, Consultation and Representation) Act 1986.** This assessment looks at whether the person needs any of the specific services listed in **The Chronically Sick and Disabled Persons Act 1970** and so is service-led:-

- practical help in the home;
- help with the provision of radio, television and telephone;
- adaptations to the home;
- assistance with travel, holidays and recreational and educational facilities.

A disabled person or someone on his or her behalf has a **right** to request this assessment, independent of any community care assessment.

Guidance requires a care plan to be produced after the assessment.

Single shared assessment means that assessments may not always be carried out by local authority employees, but the ultimate responsibility for assessment remains with the local authority. Guidance says that needs should be the paramount consideration in any assessment and that unmet need should be recorded.

Guidance on Single Shared Assessment states that informed consent to the assessment should be sought from the client as part of the assessment process. Where it is not possible to obtain informed consent, every effort should be made to obtain the past views and wishes of the client and the client's interests should be safeguarded through the involvement of a legal representative, specialist worker, carer or advocate.

The Guidance also states that informed consent to information sharing should be sought from the client (in writing) as part of the assessment process. Where it is not possible to obtain informed consent, every effort should be made to obtain the past views and wishes of the client and the client's interests should be safeguarded through the involvement of a legal representative, specialist worker, carer or advocate.

The Social Work (Scotland) Act 1968 was amended in 2007 to allow services to be provided to an incapable adult without consent where it can be shown that there is a benefit to the adult and the principles in the Adults With Incapacity (Scotland) Act 2000 have been followed. This means that a person could now be admitted to a care home without the need for formal intervention under the Adults With Incapacity (Scotland) Act 2000.

5.32   The Financial Assessment

If services are to be provided, the local authority will carry out a financial assessment to ascertain how much the person can afford to pay. If residential care is to be provided, the local authority must carry out a financial assessment. **Since 1st July 2002, personal care has been free to those aged 65 and over and nursing care (in a care home) has been free to anyone who needs it. There is still a charge for accommodation and food, subject to ability to pay. Residents in homes who are self-funding get a rebate of £145 per week (residential) or £210 per week (nursing) (2002 Act). From April 2008 the figures will be £149 and £216.**

There are currently no legal thresholds for charging for home care services (but they are planned under the 2002 Act). Some local authorities set limits of £3,000 and £8,000, i.e., if the client has less than £3,000 he or she will have that capital disregarded and if the client has over £8,000 in assets, he or she will pay the full cost of home care services.

The legal thresholds for residential care are £12,500 and £20,750, but income is also taken into account. If the client has less than £12,500 in capital, that will be disregarded. Between £12,500 and £20,750, some of the capital is taken into account. If the client has over £20,750 in capital, the client must pay the full cost of residential care.

Personal items such as furniture and jewellery are not taken into account.

The provision of services and the charging for them are 2 quite separate issues. Services may not be withdrawn, if the client refuses to pay, rather the local authority must take steps to recover the debt.

Only assets belonging to the client should can be assessed and since October 2007 the local authority is NOT entitled to ask for details of the spouse's assets or to ask that spouse to contribute towards the costs. If the client refuses to give financial information, he or she will be charged as if they can afford to pay the full cost until such time as they disclose the information.

5.33 Special Rules Relating to Charges for Residential Care

If a person deliberately, with the intent of avoiding charges, transfers an asset to a third party for no value or for less than the true value, the local authority may treat the transferor as if they still have the asset. This is known as "notional capital" and means that the local authority may continue to charge the person, even after their real assets fall below £12,500.

If the transfer took place in the 6 month period before entering residential care or during the stay in residential care, the transferee may be asked by the local authority to pay some of the charges.

The local authority is entitled to put a charging order on the property of a person receiving residential care, if that person is not paying the charges. This means that the debt is secured on the property and the local authority will receive its money when the property is sold. The 2002 Act also makes provision for the client to enter into a deferred payment agreement.

However, a house is **not** always assessable. It must be disregarded if: the following people remain living in it:-
- the partner or spouse;
- a relative over 60;
- a relative of any age who is incapacitated.

The house is also disregarded if the stay in residential care is temporary.

There is a **discretion** to disregard the house if a third party is living there because he or she gave up his or her own accommodation, in order to care for the client.

Guidance on Single Shared Assessment makes it clear that NHS services are free, but local authorities may charge for services such as residential and domiciliary care, other than aspects classified as free personal care. Charges for services should be made clear in any material produced and should be clearly explained to users as part of their assessment. The care plan should include a written explanation of any charges, and users should be advised of their rights to make representations.

5.34   The Carer's Assessment (Section 12AA and 12AB of the 1968 Act inserted by the 2002 Act)

A carer (including someone under 16) has a right to request an assessment of his or her ability to continue caring for the person who is receiving a community care assessment and the local authority has a **duty** to carry out this assessment. From September 2002 the law has been amended to allow carers to have an assessment even if the person for whom they care is not being assessed at the same time. There is also a **duty** to advise carers that they have a right to an assessment. Guidance makes it clear that the carer's assessment should be about willingness and capacity to care and that there should be no presumptions about whether a carer should provide care.

5.35　Complaints

If a client is unhappy about any part of the assessments or any decisions taken as a result, he or she may complain through the local authority complaints procedure which deals with any complaints about the social work function.

5.36　The Social Work (S) Act 1968
　　　(Choice of Accommodation) Directions 1993

The client has a **right** to choose which establishment he or she wishes to enter and has a right to be offered a temporary place in another establishment until a place becomes available in the establishment of choice.

5.37　Compulsory Removal From Home Under The
　　　National Assistance Act 1948

If a person is unable to take proper care of himself or herself and is not being properly cared for by someone else and is either:-

- suffering from a serious illness *or*
- is aged, infirm or physically incapacitated and living in insanitary conditions.

then an application may be made to the Sheriff to have that person removed to hospital or a residential setting.

A doctor must certify that it is necessary to remove the person:-

- in his or her own interests *or*
- to prevent injury to the health of other people *or*
- to prevent serious nuisance to other people

The local authority has a duty to look after the property of a person who is compulsorily removed from home.

5.38　Direct Payments – Section 12B and 12C of the 1968
　　　Act (as amended by the 2002 Act)

Since April 2004 a person over the age of 65 who is assessed as needing community care services has been eligible for direct payments whether or not they are disabled. The following service users are also entitled to direct payments:

---

a.   Disabled adults to purchase community care services
b.   Disabled people aged 16 and 17 to purchase children's services
c.   Disabled people with parental responsibility to purchase the children's services their children have been assessed as needing
d.   Parents and people with parental responsibility for a disabled child to purchase the services the disabled child has been assessed as needing
e.   Children in need
f.   Disabled adults and 16 and 17 year olds to purchase housing support services
g.   Attorneys and guardians, with the relevant powers can receive direct payments on behalf of people who are unable to give consent to arranging their own services.

Those community care service users aged 65 or over who are accessing Free Personal and Nursing Care can arrange for the personal care element of the package to be made as a direct payment.

National Guidance on Self-Directed Support can be found at:
http://www.scotland.gov.uk/Publications/2007/07/04093127/0

5.39   The Regulation of Care (S) Act 2001
This Act creates the following:

The Scottish Social Services Council became operational in October 2001. From April 2002 it has regulated the workforce by means of registration of staff and the production of codes of practice.
The Scottish Commission for the Regulation of Care became operational in April 2002 and took over the registration and inspection of care services. These services are regulated against national care standards for each client group. The Commission also deals with complaints about establishments.

The Act also gives authority for the production of National Care Standards. The key themes in the standards are dignity, privacy, choice, safety, realizing potential, equality and diversity. They are addressed to the individual and set out his or her rights.

The following National Standards are used by the Care Commission to assess services:

- Adoption Services
- Foster care and Family Placement Services
- Adult Placement Services
- Housing Support Services
- Support Services
- Short Breaks and Respite Care
- Nurse Agencies
- Care Homes for People With Drug and Alcohol Problems
- Criminal Justice Supported Accommodation Services
- Care Homes for People With Physical and Sensory Impairment
- Care Homes for People With Mental Health Problems
- Care Homes for People With Learning Disabilities
- Care at Home
- Care Homes for Older People
- Independent Hospitals
- Independent Specialist Clinics
- Dental Services
- Hospice Care
- Care Homes for Children and Young People
- Early Education and Childcare up to Age 16
- School Care Accommodation Services

The following example from The National Care Standards for Care Homes for People With Learning Disabilities gives an idea of how the standards are constructed – note that they are addressed to the client, not the establishment:

- You have the right to make decisions about your life and the care you receive;
- Unless there are legal reasons for you not to do so, you can carry out your own financial, legal and other personal business at a time that suits you;
- You can decide who should know about and have access to your personal business;
- Confidential information about you is only shared with others if you give permission, unless the law requires otherwise;
- You can see for yourself that your records are kept confidential and that access to them is only allowed in controlled circumstances;
- You can keep control of your personal belongings and money, unless legal arrangements have been made to look after them for you;

- You have a chance to spend your money in a way that lets you do the things you want;
- You have the right to choose the risks you want to take, subject to the need to ensure the safety of others;
- If you are unable to make decisions for yourself, The Adults With Incapacity (S) Act 2000 will apply;
- The staff must always respect and actively promote your rights;
- You have the right to speak for yourself and other people may only speak for you with your permission;
- The views of others should never be represented as your own;
- If you need help to make informed choices, you may wish to appoint an advocate to help you. It is important that everyone understands the distinction between speaking on your behalf and expressing a personal or professional view;
- If you are capable of understanding that you need to take medication and what will happen if you do not do so, but you refuse to take it, staff must respect your wishes.

5.4 Adult Protection

The Adult Support and Protection (S) Act 2007 was passed by the Scottish Parliament in early 2007 and the following provisions to protect "adults at risk" are expected to come into force in late 2008.

5.40 Local authority duties and powers

Duties

- To investigate the well-being, property and financial affairs of a person where it knows or believes:
  (a) that the person is an adult at risk, ***and***
  (b) that it might need to intervene in order to protect the person's well-being, property or financial affairs (s. 4)

- To have regard to the importance of the provision of appropriate services (including, in particular, independent advocacy services) to the adult concerned where it has investigated and identified a need to intervene to protect an adult at risk. (s. 6)

- To establish a committee (an "Adult Protection Committee") with the following functions:
  (a) to keep under review the procedures and practices of the public bodies and office-holders relating to the safeguarding of adults at risk present in the council's area
  (b) to give information or advice, or make proposals, to any public body and office-holder on the exercise of functions which relate to the safeguarding of adults at risk present in the council's area
  (c) to make, or assist in or encourage the making of, arrangements for improving the skills and knowledge of officers or employees of the public bodies and office-holders who have responsibilities relating to the safeguarding of adults at risk present in the council's area

Powers

- A council officer may enter any place for the purpose of enabling or assisting a council conducting inquiries under section 4 to decide whether it needs to do anything in order to protect an adult at risk from harm (s.7)

- A council officer, and any person accompanying the officer, may interview, in private, any adult found in a place being visited under section 7. An adult is not required to answer any question (and the adult must be informed of that fact before the interview starts). (s. 8)
- A council officer may require any person holding health, financial or other records relating to an individual whom the officer knows or believes to be an adult at risk to give the records, or copies of them, to the officer. (S. 10)

A health professional may conduct a medical examination of an adult where it is known or believed that the adult is at risk, subject to the adult's right to refuse, if competent to do so. (s. 9)

5.41   Defintion of "adults at risk"

"Adults at risk" are adults who

    a)   are unable to safeguard their own well-being, property, rights or other interests

    b)   are at risk of harm, ***and***

    c)   because they are affected by disability, mental disorder, illness or physical or mental infirmity, are more vulnerable to being harmed than adults who are not so affected.

The Act introduces new orders to protect adults at risk and the general principle on intervention in an adult's affairs is that a person may intervene, or authorise an intervention, only if satisfied that the intervention

    a)   will provide benefit to the adult which could not reasonably be provided without intervening in the adult's affairs, ***and***

    b)   is, of the range of options likely to fulfil the object of the intervention, the least restrictive to the adult's freedom

5.42   Assessment Order ss.11-13

The local authority may apply to the sheriff court for this order. If the sheriff grants the assessment order he must also grant a warrant for entry.

The court must take into account:

    a)   the general principle on intervention in an adult's affairs,

    b)   the adult's ascertainable wishes and feelings (past and present),

    c)   any views of-
        (i) the adult's nearest relative
        (ii) any primary carer, guardian or attorney of the adult, ***and***
        (iii) any other person who has an interest in the adult's well-being or property,

    d)   the importance of-
        (i) the adult participating as fully as possible in the performance of the function, ***and***
        (ii) providing the adult with such information and support as is necessary to enable the adult to so participate,

    e)   the importance of ensuring that the adult is not, without justification, treated less favourably than the way in which any other adult (not being an adult at risk) might be treated in a comparable situation, ***and***

f)   the adult's abilities, background and characteristics (including the adult's age, sex, sexual orientation, religious persuasion, racial origin, ethnic group and cultural and linguistic heritage).

The sheriff may only grant an assessment order if satisfied that:

a)   the local authority has reasonable cause to suspect that the person in respect of whom the order is sought is an adult at risk who is being, or is likely to be, seriously harmed

b)   that the assessment order is required in order to establish whether the person is an adult at risk who is being, or is likely to be, seriously harmed, *and*

c)   as to the availability and suitability of the place at which the person is to be interviewed and examined

The order authorises an authorised person to interview the adult in private and to carry out a medical examination in private for the purpose of establishing:

a)   whether the person is an adult at risk, *and*
b)   if it decides that the person is an adult at risk, whether it needs to do anything in order to protect the person from harm

An adult may only be removed from a place if it is not practicable to carry out a private interview or medical examination in that place. An adult must be informed of his or her right to refuse to answer any question and to refuse medical examination before the interview or examination takes place,
The order lasts for 7 days from the date of the order.

The sheriff must not make an assessment order if the sheriff knows that the affected adult at risk has refused to consent to the granting of the order and a person must not take any action for the purposes of carrying out or enforcing an assessment order if the person knows that the affected adult at risk has refused to consent to the action.

A refusal to consent may be ignored if the sheriff or person reasonably believes

(a)   that the affected adult at risk has been unduly pressurised to refuse consent, *and*

(b)   that there are no steps which could reasonably be taken with the adult's consent which would protect the adult from the harm which the order or action is intended to prevent.

5.43   Removal Order: ss.14-18

The local authority may apply to the sheriff court for this order. If the sheriff grants a removal order he must also grant a warrant for entry.

The court must take into account:

a)   the general principle on intervention in an adult's affairs,
b)   the adult's ascertainable wishes and feelings (past and present),
c)   any views of-
    a.   the adult's nearest relative
    b.   any primary carer, guardian or attorney of the adult, *and*
    c.   any other person who has an interest in the adult's well-being or property,
d)   the importance of-
    (i)   the adult participating as fully as possible in the performance of the function, *and*
    (ii)   providing the adult with such information and support as is necessary to enable the adult to so participate,
e)   the importance of ensuring that the adult is not, without justification, treated less favourably than the way in which any other adult (not being an adult at risk) might be treated in a comparable situation, *and*
f)   the adult's abilities, background and characteristics (including the adult's age, sex, sexual orientation, religious persuasion, racial origin, ethnic group and cultural and linguistic heritage).

The sheriff may only grant a removal order if satisfied:

a)   that the person in respect of whom the order is sought is an adult at risk who is likely to be seriously harmed if not moved to another place, *and*
b)   as to the availability and suitability of the place to which the adult at risk is to be moved

The order authorises a local authority officer or nominee to move a specified person to a specified place within 72 hours of the order being made, and the local authority to take such reasonable steps as it thinks fit for the purpose of protecting the moved person from harm.

The order may contain a requirement that the local authority allow a specified person to have contact with the adult at risk.

A removal order expires 7 days (or such shorter period as may be specified in the order) after the day on which the specified person is moved in pursuance of the order. The sheriff may vary or recall the order on application by the adult at risk to whom the order relates, any person who has an interest in the adult at risk's well-being or property, or the local authority.

The sheriff must not make a removal order if the sheriff knows that the affected adult at risk has refused to consent to the granting of the order and a person must not take any action for the purposes of carrying out or enforcing a removal order if the person knows that the affected adult at risk has refused to consent to the action.

A refusal to consent may be ignored if the sheriff or person reasonably believes
- (a) that the affected adult at risk has been unduly pressurised to refuse consent, *and*
- (b) that there are no steps which could reasonably be taken with the adult's consent which would protect the adult from the harm which the order or action is intended to prevent.

5.44 Banning Order: ss.19-34

The local authority must apply for a banning order if satisfied that the grounds for the order exist and no one else is likely to apply and no other court action to ban the person is pending.

An application may also be made by or on behalf of:

- a) an adult whose well-being or property would be safeguarded by the order
- b) any other person who is entitled to occupy the place concerned.

Application is made to the sheriff court.

The sheriff may also grant a temporary banning order.

The court must have regard to:

a) the general principle on intervention in an adult's affairs,
b) the adult's ascertainable wishes and feelings (past and present),
c) any views of-
   a. the adult's nearest relative
   b. any primary carer, guardian or attorney of the adult, *and*
   c. any other person who has an interest in the adult's well-being or property,
d) the importance of-
   (i) the adult participating as fully as possible in the performance of the function, *and*
   (ii) providing the adult with such information and support as is necessary to enable the adult to so participate,
e) the importance of ensuring that the adult is not, without justification, treated less favourably than the way in which any other adult (not being an adult at risk) might be treated in a comparable situation, *and*
f) the adult's abilities, background and characteristics (including the adult's age, sex, sexual orientation, religious persuasion

The court may only grant the order if satisfied:

a) that an adult at risk is being, or is likely to be, seriously harmed by another person,
b) that the adult at risk's well-being or property would be better safeguarded by banning that other person from a place occupied by the adult than it would be by moving the adult from that place, *and*
c) that either
   (i) the adult at risk is entitled, or permitted by a third party, or
   (ii) neither the adult at risk nor the subject is entitled, or permitted by a third party to occupy the place from which the subject is to be banned

A banning order bans the subject of the order from being in a specified place. It may also:

a) ban the subject from being in a specified area in the vicinity of the specified place,

b) authorise the summary ejection of the subject from the specified place and the specified area

c) prohibit the subject from moving any specified thing from the specified place

d) direct any specified person to take specified measures to preserve any moveable property owned or controlled by the subject which remains in the specified place while the order has effect

e) be made subject to any specified conditions

f) require or authorise any person to do, or to refrain from doing, anything else which the sheriff thinks necessary for the proper enforcement of the order

The sheriff may attach a power of arrest to the banning order and a constable may arrest a person who breaches the order without a warrant.

The order may last for a maximum of 6 months or such shorter period as the court may impose. The sheriff may vary or recall the order on application by the subject to the order, the applicant for the order, the adult at risk or any person who can show an interest.

The sheriff must not make a banning order or temporary banning order if the sheriff knows that the affected adult at risk has refused to consent to the granting of the order and a person must not take any action for the purposes of carrying out or enforcing a banning order or temporary banning order if the person knows that the affected adult at risk has refused to consent to the action.

A refusal to consent may be ignored if the sheriff or person reasonably believes

(a) that the affected adult at risk has been unduly pressurised to refuse consent, *and*

(b) that there are no steps which could reasonably be taken with the adult's consent which would protect the adult from the harm which the order or action is intended to prevent.

5.45 The Protection of Vulnerable Groups (Scotland) Act 2007

When this Act is brought into force it will create a list of persons unsuitable to work with adults. The new adults' list and the pre-existing children's list will be managed by a Central Barring Unit (CBU). The effect of being listed in Scotland, i.e. included on the adults' list or children's list, is that an individual is barred from undertaking that type of regulated work in Scotland (or regulated activity anywhere else in the UK) and risks imprisonment if they do so. Similarly, any individual listed by the Independent Safeguarding Authority in England is barred from doing regulated work in Scotland.

Part Six

Negligence, Consent, Conflict of Interest and Advocacy

Part Six

Negligence, Consent, Conflict of Interest and Advocacy

6.0   Negligence

In legal terms, negligence is the failure of a person to act with the required level of care or to fail to do something they ought to have done, as the result of which a person has suffered loss.

A person who suffers loss or damage directly due to the negligence of another, can raise a civil court action to seek compensation for the loss caused, referred to as damages. An award of damages by the court will be made against the employer, for example the health Board, rather than the individual professional.

As a health professional, even if a legal action for negligence is unsuccessful, the NMC or GMC may still take disciplinary action.

6.10   The Duty of Care
In terms of the health profession, the level of care required is that of the ordinary, competent health professional of a similar position. In other words the standard expected varies, and would be greater if the health professional has a position of greater responsibility.

It is important to note that a health care professional who performs a procedure, beyond the scope of their duties, for which they have not the skill or training, will nonetheless be judged to the standard of a competent professional in carrying out the task. For example, a student nurse should refuse to carry out a procedure that they are not trained for and are not being adequately supervised.

To determine the level of skill and care that could be expected from the ordinary competent professional the court may hear evidence from expert witness, and may be referred to professional body publications. So, for example, the court

---

would most probably be referred to the NMC Standards for the Administration of Medicines in the event of an allegation of injury due to an injection having been badly administered.

In some cases the opinion as to the correct approach to a procedure may be divided in the profession. The fact that some members of the profession take an alternative view of the correct action, does not make the chosen method negligent.

As the level of care is that of the ordinary competent member of the profession, not that of *'super nurse'*, not all errors of judgement will in law amount to negligence. The circumstances surrounding the event will always be examined in the courts, hence the need to ensure that adequate records have been kept, explaining why particular decisions have been made. The courts will be looking to establish whether the nurse acted reasonably in the circumstances.

6.11   Acting Reasonably in the Circumstances

Where the health professional is acting in the course of their employment, the standard that they are expected to carry out their duties to is that of a competent professional of their position. Therefore for a nurse employed by a Health Board to work on a ward, whilst on that Ward they must act to the standard expected of a nurse of their position (which should reflect their expertise and experience). However away from the ward the standard of care is lower, because they are no longer operating in the field of expertise or responsibility.

Due to the professional responsibility of a health care professional, although not legally required to intervene in events outwith their employment, they are likely to feel professionally obligated to assist if they come across an incident. In such circumstances the professional is expected to act to the best of their knowledge and experience only, and not that of a specialist.

6.12   Consent To Treatment

One of the most common issues in negligence claims is the issue of whether the patient's consent was obtained prior to treatment.

Generally a patient may refuse to undergo treatment or may withdraw their consent to continued treatment at any time.

Therefore the patient's wishes should be respected, even if their refusal is based on non-medical factors, such as refusal of treatment on the grounds of religious belief. Where a patient refuses treatment this must be adequately recorded, and if possible it should be witnessed.

It is a criminal assault on a person to carry out treatment unless they have freely consented except in an emergency situation. It is also a breach of Article 8 of the European Convention on Human Rights – the right to respect for private life.

Children Under 16

In Part 3 it was explained that for a child under the age of 16, the consent of the parents is not required where in the opinion of the medical practitioner the child is capable of understanding the nature and consequences of the procedure (**Age of Legal Capacity (S) Act 1991).** Where the child does not have such understanding the consent of a person with parental responsibilities and rights is required.

If the young person is capable of giving consent, then their decision to refuse treatment cannot be overridden by the person with parental responsibilities and rights.

If there is no one with parental responsibilities and rights available, a person with care or control of a child may give medical consent **if** the child is unable to consent or refuse **and** if a person with parental responsibilities and rights would not object. **(Section 5 Children (S) Act 1995)**.

If there is a dispute about medical treatment, any person claiming interest may apply to the sheriff for a specific issue order under **Section 11 of The Children (S) Act 1995.**

Patient 16 years and Over

No person, including a parent or relative, has the automatic right to give consent for another adult. A person appointed as a welfare guardian may have been given the authority by a sheriff to give medical consent on behalf of the person they are appointed to act for. Prior to losing capacity to consent, a person may have signed a welfare power of attorney which may give another person authority to give medical consent. If there is no one legally authorized to give medical consent, doctors may treat the patient without consent after completing certain formalities under The Adults With Incapacity (S) Act 2000. A patient may also be treated without consent if detained under **The Mental Health (Care and Treatment) (S) Act 2003**, but only treatment for the mental disorder may be given.

How To Ascertain If the Patient Is Capable of Giving Informed Consent Or Refusal?

- The patient must be able to take in the information and retain it long enough to weigh up the options;
- The patient must believe and understand the information;
- The patient must be able to make a free and informed choice.

6.13   Requirement to Inform

To obtain a patient's informed consent it is necessary that he or she is in the position to make an informed decision.

Therefore, it is necessary to explain to the patient:

- any choice of procedure that may exist;
- the medical professional's recommended treatment, and the reasons for their selected method of treatment;
- the nature of the treatment, any likely side effects or risks. Where the treatment involves any unusual or substantial risk such as in surgery or radiation treatment, these risks must be explained. In all other circumstances, it is a matter of professional judgement as to what risks to disclose and the terms of warning.

It is also imperative to explain to the patient that he or she does not have to agree to any treatment or procedure. Some patients may otherwise feel unable to refuse.

The level of detail that should be given to the patient will depend on the assessment of the situation by the health professional and should include the state of the patient- are they in shock, pain or distress, do they speak English as a first language.

It is important to remember that a patient being treated for a mental disorder may nonetheless still be in a position to consent to the proposed treatment.

6.14   Recording the Giving of Consent

It is not necessary to get consent in writing. However where consent has been given orally, this should be recorded. For treatments involving substantial risk or side effects, written consent should be obtained. The NHS Management Executive has devised model consent sheets for use where written consent is required.
Note that even where a patient has signed a consent form, this will not be sufficient protection against a claim for negligence if the risks of the treatment were not properly explained.

6.15   Overriding the Need for Consent

Whilst a patient generally has the right to withdraw from treatment, treatment may be administered without consent in limited circumstances:

- For lifesaving procedures where the patient is unconscious or unable to give their consent or in the case of a child under 16 where there is insufficient time to obtain the consent of the parent and the child is unable to consent;
- Where the procedure is authorised by a statutory power, although even then the consent should still be sought;
- Treatment for the mental disorder of a detained patient, as detailed in Part 5.

6.2   Conflict of Interest

6.20   Conscientious Objection

In the event that due to a matter of conscientious objection a health care professional is not prepared to undertake certain procedures, then this should be notified to the appropriate person or body at the earliest opportunity.

However, generally it is expected that a health care professional will treat each patient with dignity and without discrimination.

In strict legal terms the only situations where a health care professional has a legal right to refuse to participate in any treatment is in connection with either

- abortion *or*

- fertilisation - technological procedures to achieve conception and pregnancy.

This right not to participate in such procedures does not remove the duty of the health care professional to participate in any treatment that is necessary to save the life of or to prevent serious permanent injury of a pregnant woman. Therefore if an emergency in an abortion procedure were to occur, a nurse could not refuse to take part in the emergency treatment or to provide the necessary care.

If legal proceedings were to arise from a situation where a health care professional had refused to participate, the professional would have to satisfy the court that they had a relevant conscientious objection.

6.21 Withdrawal of Treatment for Protection of Yourself or the Public

The duty to provide care in a non-discriminatory manner may come into conflict with the principle to ensure safe practice where the behaviour of the patient is likely to result in physical violence or has health and safety implications.

Other behaviour such as sexual or racial harassment may also put the health care professional in a conflict situation. However judgement as to whether the individual's illness was self-inflicted, such as smoking, should not affect the availability of treatment.

In all these cases it is essential that both the management and the patient's family are fully advised as to why treatment is being withdrawn. It may also be appropriate to advise the patient also. It is important that adequate records are kept of the reasons for the decision and the discussions held so that these are available if the event of a complaint.

6.22 Patients Refusing or Seeking Withdrawal of Treatment Where Death/ Serious Injury Likely

A conflict of interest can arise when a patient or their representatives refuse to accept treatment even although a consequence of their refusal is likely to be serious, even resulting in death. The conflict is to determine whether the prolonging of life is in the patient's best interests and whether their consent should be dispensed with.

Common difficult areas include the religious objection to blood transfusions by Jehovah's Witnesses, issues of force feeding those with mental disorders such as anorexia and the termination of life sustaining treatments for those in a persistent vegetative state.

When an adult patient in a critical condition refuses essential medical treatment, then generally their decision must be respected. The fact that a patient has a mental impairment does not prevent them from refusing treatment for other aliments, including the right to refuse treatment even where death or serious injury may result.

However, it is important to consider whether the patient's capacity to make a decision has been affected by confusion, pain or shock or whether the patient's independent will has been overcome by someone else's undue influence. Where there is doubt about a person's ability to consent, two medical reports should be sought from treating doctors, psychiatrists or the GP. If these medical reports disclose a real doubt as to the validity of the patient's refusal, in the public interest the health authorities should apply to the court for an order to enable treatment.

Unconscious Patients and Advance Directives
Although the patient may have become unconscious, their general right to consent to or refuse treatment still exists. Therefore if the patient had made an advance directive whilst lucid, then the directive should normally be taken into account. This can be of particular importance for midwives as some women elect not to undergo caesarean sections in their birth plans. In law the foetus does not have any rights, and therefore decisions of the mother are paramount.

Children
Where a patient is a young person under the age of 16 but is able to give their consent, they have the same ability to refuse lifesaving treatment as they have to agree to treatment.

Where the young person is not capable of giving consent, consent from the person with parental responsibilities and rights will be sought. In the event that the person with parental responsibilities and rights refuses consent for life saving procedures or where is a clear risk of serious permanent harm, the medical profession is not bound by that decision. The matter should be discussed with the parent in the presence of a medical colleague, who should countersign the record. Where the child is in an emergency situation, whether treatment is carried out will be a matter of professional competence and conscience, involving a judgement on what is in the best interests of the patient. Otherwise the Health Authority may petition the court to allow the treatment to be given. The court will decide on the basis of what it considers to be in the best interests of the child. A child protection order may also give authority for medical examination or treatment, but may not override a competent refusal by a child.

6.23   Patient Interests and Loyalty to Colleagues/ Employers

Conflicts may arise where due to the broad duties on a health care professional to act in the best interests of the patient, they come into conflict with the interest of colleagues or management. One such occasion where such conflict is possible is that of advocacy, which is discussed below. Another possibility is where the health care professional is of the opinion that a colleague or colleagues have acted or are acting in a grossly inappropriate manner. As discussed in Part 2, the Public Interest Disclosure Act 1998 provides protection for an employee who reports another where it appears it is likely that the one of the following has occurred and is being or is likely to be concealed:

- that a criminal offence has occurred;
- that a person has failed, is failing or is likely to fail to comply with any legal obligation;
- that a miscarriage of justice has occurred, is occurring or is likely to occur;
- that the health or safety of any individual has been, is being or is likely to be endangered;
- that the environment has been, is being or is likely to be damaged, or
- that information tending to show any matter falling into any of the above categories has been or is likely to be deliberately concealed.

In such circumstances the duty of loyalty to employers and colleagues is outweighed by public interest in the disclosure of this information.

6.24   Refusal of Treatment and Human Rights

Article 2 of the European Convention on Human Rights gives the right to life. There have been a number of reports in the recent past about certain patients being denied medical treatment. No one doubts that the NHS has to use its restricted funds very carefully, but what is now clear is that The Human Rights Act 1998 will not permit arbitrary decisions about who may receive treatment, particularly if those decisions are based on discrimination. For example, a refusal to treat patients with learning disability, either due to their inability to consent or even worse, due to judgements about the value of treating these patients, could be a breach of Article 2, if that refusal of treatment would result in death, and a breach of Article 14, if the refusal to treat amounts to a failure to apply the rights in The European Convention on Human Rights to every citizen without discrimination. It is worth noting that access to medical treatment would include access to screening programmes. In addition, care will be needed about "do not resuscitate" orders.

The key to defending any human rights challenge will be evidence of a proper prioritizing of need and proper recording of how and why decisions were made. The British Medical Association has issued guidance to doctors on the care needed in making decisions about whether to treat. The guidance reminds doctors that "issues such as human dignity, communication and consultation, and best interests which are central to good clinical practice are also pivotal to the Convention rights". It also stresses that decisions taken about individual patients and medical policy must take account of Convention rights and be transparent and able to withstand scrutiny. Clearly, in order to defend any human rights challenge, it will be necessary for accurate and adequate records to be made at the time of any decision.

6.3   Advocacy

Advocacy is linked with patient choice, and requires the health care professional to ensure the patient receives the treatment option that they chose (or in some cases that the treatment is withdrawn). Advocacy is part of the general scope of the nursing and health care professionals' duties.

In the context of the health care profession, it means promoting and protecting the interests of the patients or clients, especially where the patient may be vulnerable due to either age or mental impairment.

Advocacy involves providing patients with appropriate information about their treatment, the choices available, and ensuring that they feel empowered, as far, as is possible in their circumstances, to make their own decision. Advocacy offers support to a patient at a time when they may feel anxious, thereby reducing stress and perhaps leading to better results.

6.30   Health Professional as Advocate

When a health care professional acts in the role of an advocate for a patient, they may feel under some pressure from colleagues. The role of the advocate often involves asking more questions, requiring other colleagues to take more time to explain matters and may involve supporting a patient who decides not to accept the recommended treatment. It is important that the health care professional considers such potential conflict. Where conflict is likely to occur, the health care professional may wish to recommend an independent advocacy service to the patient.

6.31   Independent Advocates

The Patient's Charter in Scotland recognises that all users of health services have a right to advocacy. The Mental Health (Care and Treatment) (S) Act 2003 gives a person with a mental disorder a legal right to an independent advocate.

Advocacy may be carried out by health care professionals, such as the patient's named-nurse, or it may be a carried out by an independent service. An independent advocate's role is to help the patient to put forward his or her views. The advocate may not advise the patient or make decisions on behalf of the patient.

In addition, for some patients there may be formally appointed persons to look after the patient's interests. A child may have a safeguarder appointed by the court or the Children's Panel. The role of the safeguarder is to report to the Panel or the court on what is in the best interests of the child. This is clearly a different role to that of an independent advocate.

It should be remembered that if a patient has consented to the disclosure of confidential information to their advocate (or anyone else), then disclosure of relevant information can be made - after all, the role of the advocate is to help and support the patient.

Part Seven
Human Rights and the U.N. Convention on the Rights of the Child

Article 2	The Right to Life
Article 3	Freedom From Inhuman or Degrading Treatment
Article 4	Prohibition on Forced Labour
Article 5	The Right to Liberty
Article 6	The Right to a Fair Hearing
Article 8	The Right to Respect for Private and Family Life, Home and Correspondence
Article 9	The Right to Freedom of Thought, Conscience and Religion
Article 10	The Right to Freedom of Expression
Article 14	The Right to Enjoy the Convention Rights Without Discrimination

First Protocol

Article 2	The Right to Education

The UN Convention on the Rights of the Child

Part Seven

Human Rights and the U.N. Convention on the Rights of the Child

The Human Rights Act 1998 came into force in October 2000. It has the following effects:

- It incorporates the European Convention on Human Rights into national law;
- It allows victims of a human rights breach to raise a case in a national court up to one year after the alleged breach;
- It requires legislation to be interpreted as far as possible in accordance with the rights set down in the Convention;
- It makes it unlawful for a public authority to act or to fail to act in a manner that is inconsistent with the rights set down in the Convention.

The question of the application of the Human Rights Act 1998 to private care homes has recently been the subject of litigation in England & Wales. The Court of Appeal in Johnson & Ors v. Havering London Borough Council [2007] followed the decision in the previous Leonard Cheshire case and concluded that a private care home was not performing the functions of a public authority under the Human Rights Act 1998. The court did however make it clear that a Local Authority's statutory obligations in the provision of a care home place provide continued protection for service users in these situations that extend beyond the scope of human rights claims. Whilst this case law does not set a precedent in Scotland, it does provide some clarity on the division of responsibility between local authorities and private providers of residential care. The local authority is not relieved of their responsibility in these matters by the transfer of care homes to private control. The UK government has indicated that it may change the law to allow private care homes to be brought within the provisions of the Human Rights Act 1998

If you work for a health board or trust, you should consider the human rights implications whenever making decisions. You should be particularly careful when exercising discretion in decision-making processes. As individuals can bring a case against your employer up to one year after the alleged breach, adequate recording of why and how decisions were made is essential.

The rights will now be considered in detail with some comment on how they may affect your practice. Some rights are absolute and some allow for interference, but only when it can be objectively justified.

Article 2 :   The Right to Life

Everyone's right to life shall be protected by law. Deprivation of life shall not be regarded as inflicted in contravention of this Article when it results from the use of force which is no more than absolutely necessary:
   a)   in the defence of any person from unlawful violence;
   b)   in order to effect a lawful arrest or to prevent the escape of a
         person lawfully detained;
   c)   in action lawfully taken for the purpose of quelling a riot or
         insurrection.

Under the Human Rights Act 1998, public authorities have a duty to protect life. This is likely to have the following implications for practice:

The Refusal of Medical Treatment
There have been a number of reports in the recent past about certain patients being denied medical treatment. No one doubts that the NHS has to use its restricted funds very carefully, but what is now clear is that The Human Rights Act 1998 will not permit arbitrary decisions about who may receive treatment, particularly if those decisions are based on discrimination. For example, a refusal to treat patients with learning disability, either due to their inability to consent or even worse, due to judgements about the value of treating these patients, could be a breach of Article 2, if that refusal of treatment would result in death, and a breach of Article 14, if the refusal to treat amounts to a failure to apply the rights in The European Convention on Human Rights to every citizen without discrimination. It is worth noting that access to medical treatment would include access to screening programmes. In addition, care will be needed about "do not resuscitate" orders.

The key to defending any human rights challenge will be evidence of a proper prioritizing of need and proper recording of how and why decisions were made.

The British Medical Association has issued guidance to doctors on the care needed in making decisions about whether to treat. The guidance reminds doctors that "issues such as human dignity, communication and consultation, and best interests which are central to good clinical practice are also pivotal to the Convention rights". It also stresses that decisions taken about individual patients and medical policy must take account of Convention rights and be transparent and able to withstand scrutiny. Clearly, in order to defend any human rights challenge, it will be necessary for accurate and adequate records to be made at the time of any decision.

Article 3 : Freedom From Torture, Inhuman or Degrading Treatment

This right is absolute and allows for no exceptions. However, for treatment to be inhuman or degrading it must reach a high level of severity. The European Court has said that treatment which causes "intense physical or mental suffering" comes within this category, as does treatment which "arouses in the victim feelings of fear, anguish and inferiority capable of humiliating and debasing him and possibly breaking his physical or moral resistance".

This raises the following practical issues:

1. **Abuse or neglect in residential homes, nursing homes or by people providing domiciliary care.**
   If these services are provided by or on behalf of a local authority or health authority, this could now be challenged under Article 3. In one case, leaving a client in soiled clothing overnight was held by the European Court of Human Rights to be a breach of Article 3.

2. **Bullying whether involving children, young people or adults.**
   In relation to children and young people suffering bullying at school, there is very clear guidance on the measures which schools are expected to take to deal with bullying. If the education authority did not take adequate steps to tackle bullying and the child or young person suffered inhuman or degrading treatment as a result, that could be a breach of Article 3.

   In relation to adults who are in the care of a public authority, bullying by staff or others could fall within the scope of Article 3.

3. **Physical restraint.**

Physical restraint may only be used when necessary to protect a person from injuring himself or other people and the amount of force used must be no more than is reasonable in the circumstances. If physical restraint goes beyond what is reasonable, the person carrying out the restraint could be committing a criminal offence (assault) and/or may also be found liable in civil law for negligence.

In addition, a public authority which permits unreasonable physical restraint may be breaching Article 3. As well as obvious forms of physical restraint, other issues such as the use of chairs that restrain people by making it impossible for them to move or locking people in parts of an establishment may also arise. Physical restraint could also breach Article 5 - the right to liberty.

4. **Failure to protect a vulnerable child or adult from abuse.**

The European Court of Human Rights has recently given judgements in a case relating to child protection.

In the case involving Bedfordshire Council, the Court ruled that there had been a violation of Article 3 in the failure to remove four children from home despite reports of severe emotional and physical abuse. In addition, the Court found that the children had been denied an effective remedy when the House of Lords ruled that the local authority could not be held liable for its failure to act.

5. **Compulsory medical treatment.**

There are two issues under this heading. First, unless a person is detained under The Mental Health (Care and Treatment) (Scotland) Act 2003, if he or she is capable of giving medical consent, that consent must be sought.

Second, certain treatments such as force feeding or ECT may be called into question, although the European Court of Human Rights has accepted that quite severe treatment may be justified by medical necessity.

6. **Physical punishment of children.**

The law on physical punishment of children in Scotland was changed in 2003 as a result of a European Court judgement that found that

English Law did not give adequate protection from inhuman or degrading treatment in relation to physical punishment. This judgement would have to be taken into account in any cases coming before national courts. The law in Scotland now does not permit shaking, hitting on the head or the use of any implement.

It should be noted that even if treatment does not reach the threshold of "inhuman or degrading", it may still be a breach of Article 8, the right to respect for private life, since the European Court of Human Rights has held that this right includes issues relating to bodily integrity.

Article 4 : Prohibition on Forced Labour

1. No one shall be held in slavery or servitude.

2. No one shall be required to perform forced or compulsory labour.

3. For the purpose of this Article the term "forced or compulsory labour" shall not include:

    a) any work required to be done in the ordinary course of detention imposed according to the provisions of Article 5 of this Convention or during conditional release from such detention;

    b) any service of a military character or, in case of conscientious objectors in countries where they are recognized, service exacted instead of compulsory military service;

    c) any service exacted in case of an emergency or calamity threatening the life or well-being of the community;

    d) any work or service which forms part of normal civic obligations.

One practice issue that has been raised in relation to Article 4 is that of people with learning disability who are sometimes given unpaid work to do. Careful consideration should be given as to whether the nature and extent of such work requires that a contract and pay should be offered.

Article 5 :   The Right to Liberty

1. Everyone has the right to liberty and security of person. No one shall be deprived his liberty save in the following cases and in accordance with a procedure prescribed by law:

    a) the lawful detention of a person after conviction by a competent court;

    b) the lawful arrest or detention of a person for non-compliance with the lawful order of a court or in order to secure the fulfillment of any obligation prescribed by law;

    c) the lawful arrest or detention of a person effected for the purpose of bringing him before the competent legal authority on reasonable suspicion of having committed an offence or when it is reasonably considered necessary to prevent his committing an offence or fleeing after having done so;

    d) the detention of a minor by lawful order for the purpose of educational supervision or his lawful detention for the purpose of bringing him before the competent legal authority;

    e) the lawful detention of persons for the prevention of spreading infectious diseases, of persons of unsound mind, alcoholics or drug addicts or vagrants;

    f) the lawful arrest or detention of a person to prevent his effecting an unauthorized entry into the country or of a person against whom action is being taken with a view to deportation or extradition.

2. Everyone who is arrested shall be informed promptly, in a language which he understands, of the reasons for his arrest and of any charge against him.

3. Everyone arrested or detained in accordance with paragraph 1 (c) of this Article shall be brought promptly before a judge or other officer authorized by law to exercise judicial power and shall be entitled to trial within a reasonable time or to release pending trial. Release may be conditioned by guarantees to appear for trial.

4. Everyone who is deprived of his liberty by arrest or detention shall be entitled to take proceedings by which the lawfulness of his detention shall be decided speedily by a court and his release ordered if the detention is not lawful.

5. Everyone who has been the victim of arrest or detention in contravention of the provisions of this Article shall have an enforceable right to compensation.

Note that restriction of liberty **must** fall within one of the exceptions listed above and **must be carried out in accordance with law.**

Article 5 raises the following practice issues:

1. **Mental Health**
    Although mental health law is generally considered to be compatible with ECHR rights, the processes of detention and appeals and reviews will have to be rigorously applied and monitored, in order to ensure that detention remains lawful. The European Court of Human Rights has stated that:
    -   there must be an objective assessment of a mental disorder;
    -   that disorder must be serious enough to warrant detention;
    -   detention must not last longer than is necessary.

    The area where ECHR rights are likely to come into play is that of "informal detention". The majority of psychiatric patients are not detained, but have entered hospital as voluntary patients. Care will have to be exercised that such voluntary patients do not become informally detained by threats of detention.

2. **People Forced to Stay in Establishments Against Their Wishes**
    Currently there are large numbers of older people bed-blocked in hospitals awaiting provision of services in the community. It may be argued that, if there is no medical need for a person to be in hospital and that person wishes to leave, that this situation amounts to a restriction of liberty.

Some people may feel that their liberty is being restricted because they are forced to live in a residential setting when it would be possible for them to remain in the community, if resources were available. If resources are the only issue, this could amount to a breach of Article 5.

3.   **Physical Restraint**

The use of physical restraint might amount to a breach of Article 5, but it is likely that the right to liberty might have to be balanced with the duty to keep someone safe. However, the use of measures such as chairs that make it impossible for people to move around and locked doors should be carefully monitored. In addition, any restriction on the general movement of clients may have to be justified.

4.   **Refugees and Asylum Seekers**

The prolonged detention of refugees and asylum seekers might be challenged under Article 5, since they may be detained (sometimes in prison) for many months, having committed no criminal offence.

5.   **Criminal Matters**

Note that under Article 5 a person who is arrested has the right to be promptly informed of the reason *in a language that he understands.* This would not simply cover people who do not understand English, but would also cover people who use special means of communication.

Article 6:   The Right to a Fair Hearing

1.   In the determination of his civil rights and obligations or of any criminal charge against him, everyone is entitled to a fair and public hearing within a reasonable time by an independent and impartial tribunal established by law. Judgement shall be pronounced publicly but the press and public may be excluded from all or part of the trial in the interests of morals, public order or national security in a democratic society, where the interest of juveniles or the protection of the private life parties so require, or to the extent strictly necessary in the opinion of the court in special circumstances where publicity would prejudice the interests of justice.

2. Everyone charged with a criminal offence shall be presumed innocent until proved guilty according to law.

3. Everyone charged with a criminal offence has the following minimum rights:

    a) to be informed promptly, in a language which he understands and in detail, of the nature and cause of the accusation against him;
    b) to have adequate time and facilities for the preparation of his defence;
    c) To defend himself in person or through legal assistance of his own choosing or, if he has not sufficient means to pay for legal assistance, to be given it free when the interests of justice so require;
    d) To examine or have examined witnesses against him and to obtain the attendance and examination of witnesses on his behalf under the same conditions as witnesses against him;

    e) To have the free assistance of an interpreter if he cannot understand or speak the language used in court.

Article 6 guarantees the following rights:

*   Access to an independent court or tribunal;
*   A public hearing;
*   A hearing within a reasonable time;
*   Reasons for decisions.

This section concentrates on the civil aspects of Article 6 and the practice issues that may arise.

There is no definition of "civil rights and obligations", but the following are examples of some civil rights:

*   Property rights;
*   Rights affecting family life;
*   Rights to welfare benefits.

Until such time as there is clarity on how the domestic courts will interpret "civil rights and obligations", good practice and good risk management require that the principles set out in Article 6 are respected. When dealing with clients and patients, it is important that they are allowed to participate in any decision-making process and that there is "equality of arms". This means that the client or patient should not be substantially disadvantaged in relation to the public authority and will require that the client or patient is properly informed and assisted to participate.

1. Adoption
The English courts have already dealt with cases relating to the rights of an unmarried father to be notified that his child is being considered for adoption and have declared that Article 6 would normally require an unmarried father to be notified, even though that may breach the mother's right to respect for private life. (Re H and Re G [2001] 1 FLR 646). There would have to be very exceptional reasons for denying the father the right to be involved, such as threats to the safety of the mother.

There is no requirement under the Scottish Adoption Regulations for an unmarried father to be notified that his child is being considered for adoption, but the Regulations do not prohibit it. It should be borne in mind that an unmarried father may not have attended his child's children's hearing, if he is not a "relevant person" as defined in The Children (S) Act 1995 and thus may have been excluded from decisions about the child.

2. Children's Hearings
In the case of S v Miller (2001 SLT 531) (www.scotcourts.gov.uk) the Court of Session looked at various aspects of the children's hearing system in relation to human rights. The court concluded that the hearing is an independent and impartial tribunal, but the fact that legal aid is not available for legal representation has now been addressed as it would have been a breach of Article 6. The children's hearing system now has a process whereby legal representation can be made available for a child.

3. Community Care
It is unclear to what extent the provision of community care services might fall within the definition of "civil rights and obligations", but good

practice requires that the assessment process is as open and transparent as possible and that the client and other relevant persons are enabled to effectively participate in the process. Reasons for decisions should be given. There is no appeal against decisions relating to community care. It is unlikely that the social work complaints procedure meets the requirements of Article 6, but the client may seek judicial review of decisions about community care and this might be sufficient to satisfy Article 6.

4. Child Care

Issues relating to adoption have already been addressed above.

It is unclear to what extent a case conference might be determining "civil rights and obligations". However, it would be good practice to follow the requirements for fair procedure set out in Article 6. Participants should be clear about the purpose and operation of the conference and should have sufficient information. They should also be allowed to bring someone with them for support and should be allowed to see all the material to be considered by the case conference. Reasons for decisions should be clearly set out.

In any situation where decisions are to be made that might interfere with the right to respect for family life in Article 8, the requirements of Article 6 should be adhered to. Even if Article 6 does not apply to a situation, the European Court of Human Rights has declared that Article 8 also contains procedural requirements relating to fairness that must be taken into account.

5. Education

It seems likely that decisions about exclusion will be subject to the requirements in Article 6. It may be that the Appeal Committee which deals with education matters is not sufficiently independent, but the procedure could comply with the requirements of fairness. Particular attention should be paid to keeping the proceedings as informal as possible, having regard to the age and maturity of the child. It is worth noting that children in Scotland may now appeal against their own exclusion, if they have sufficient maturity.

6. Housing

It seems unlikely that Article 6 will apply to the lack of an independent appeal on decisions about homelessness. Decisions on homelessness are matters of public law and probably do not fall within the definition of "civil rights and obligations".

In general terms, employees of public authorities should consider in any situation where they **may** be determining civil rights and obligations, whether the procedures and processes would comply with the requirements of Article 6.

Article 8: Right to Respect for Private & Family Life, Home & Correspondence

1. Everyone has the right to respect for his private and family life, his home and his correspondence.

2. There shall be no interference by a public authority with the exercise of this right except such as is in accordance with law and is necessary in a democratic society in the interests of national security, public safety or the economic well-being of the country, for the prevention of disorder or crime, for the protection of health or morals, or for the protection of the rights and freedoms of others.

   This right is not absolute. Interference is permitted, but only if:

   - It is in accordance with law;
   - It pursues a legitimate aim;
   - It is supported by sufficient and relevant reasons;
   - It is proportionate to the risk observed.

The right to respect for private life

This right includes issues about confidentiality. If confidentiality is to be breached, a health professional should consider:

- The code or policy that applies in his or her workplace;
- Why confidentiality needs to be breached;
- Whether there are sufficient and relevant reasons to justify the proposed breach;
- Whether the risk observed outweighs the right to respect for private life.

It is crucial that such decisions and the way they are reached are properly recorded in sufficient detail to defend a human rights challenge up to one year after the action was taken.

The right to respect for private life also includes issues relating to "bodily integrity". A failure to take proper consent for medical treatment could breach Article 8 as could any type of ill-treatment that falls short of inhuman or degrading treatment under Article 3, but affects the person's physical integrity. It also includes issues relating to physical privacy and the right to establish and develop personal relationships.

The right to respect for family life.

This right has huge implications for childcare and child protection.

The removal of a child from home will constitute a breach of Article 8, but may be justified in the interests of the child. Section 22 of The Children (Scotland) Act 1995 requires local authorities to promote the upbringing of a child in need by his or her family, unless that is inconsistent with the welfare of the child. It might be argued that a failure to fulfill this duty for reasons relating only to resources may well breach Article 8.

The European Court of Human Rights has consistently stated that

Taking a child into care should normally be considered to be a temporary measure, and any measures to implement this temporary care should be consistent with the ultimate aim of reuniting the child and parent. A fair balance has to be struck between the interests of the child in remaining in care and those of the parent in being reunited.
(Olsson v Sweden 1988, Johanssen v Norway 1996, EP v Italy 1999, K & T v Finland 2000)

This makes it very clear that decisions about contact need to be very carefully considered. Any interference with contact must

- Be in accordance with law;
- Pursue a legitimate aim;
- Be supported by sufficient and relevant reasons;
- Be proportionate to the risk observed.

Again, recording of such decisions may be crucial to defending a human rights challenge. Although the European Court refers to balancing the interests of the child and the rights of the parents, it has accepted that sometimes the interests of the child must override the rights of the parents. However, whilst Scots and English law regard the welfare of the child as paramount, simply quoting this principle, without supporting evidence, will not be sufficient to defend a human rights challenge. The European Court has stated that a decision to terminate contact must *be justified by an overriding need in relation to the interests of the child* (Johanssen v Norway 1996). *Administrative difficulties that make contact difficult or impossible do not provide a sufficient excuse* (Olsson v Sweden 1988). Therefore, placing a child at a distance and failing to facilitate contact is likely to breach Article 8. Section 17 of The Children (Scotland) Act 1995 requires local authorities to promote contact between a looked after child and person with parental responsibilities, unless that is inconsistent with the welfare of the child. The guidance reinforces this by saying that contact should be facilitated and that financial assistance should be given. Thus national law is supporting the right in Article 8.

The European Court has also stated that

The enjoyment by parent and child of each other's company constitutes a fundamental element of family life, even where the relationship between the parents has broken down.
(Keegan v Ireland 1994)

The right to respect for family life also includes the right to be treated properly and fairly as regards procedural issues. The European Court has stated that *parents have to be involved in the decision-making process to a degree sufficient to provide them with a requisite protection of their interests. Regard may be had to the length of local authority procedures as well as to the length*

of court proceedings (W v UK 1987). Thus, even if Article 6 – the right to a fair hearing - does not apply to a particular issue because it does not involve the determination of a civil right, the procedural requirements of Article 8 will still apply. It will therefore be important to ensure that parents are invited to meetings, are properly informed about their rights and are helped to participate as effectively as possible. The Court has not yet addressed the question of whether the procedural fairness required by Article 8 applies to children, but there seems to be no reason why it should not.

In the recent decision by the European Court in T.P. & K.M. v UK there is a clear example of failure to involve a mother in the decision-making process. In this case the child was removed from her mother and the care proceedings hinged on video evidence obtained by a social worker and a child psychologist. The mother was not allowed to see the video until some 11 months later when it became clear that the child had not been referring to the mother's partner as an alleged abuser, but to another person.

The right to respect for family life does not only affect public law. Even in private law cases involving parental responsibilities and rights, national courts are already considering Article 8, since the courts are public authorities.

Finally, the right to respect for family life does not only apply to the parent/child relationship as described above. It could also apply to the situation where an elderly person was being forced to leave the family unit to enter residential care, particularly if the person could stay at home, if resources were available.

Article 9: The Right to Freedom of Thought, Conscience and Religion

> Everyone has the right to freedom of thought, conscience and religion; this right includes freedom to change his religion or belief and freedom, either alone or in community with others and in public or private, to manifest his religion or belief, in worship, teaching, practice and observance.

Freedom to manifest one's religion or beliefs shall be subject only to such limitations as are prescribed by law and are necessary in a democratic society in the interests of public safety, for the protection of public order, health or morals, or for the protection of the rights and freedoms of others.

The practical implications of this for public authorities are that they must ensure that anyone in their care is free to practice their religion, if they so wish.

Article 10: The Right To Freedom of Expression

Everyone has the right to freedom of expression. This right shall include freedom to hold opinions and to receive and impart information and ideas without interference by public authority and regardless of frontiers.

The exercise of these freedoms, since it carries with it duties and responsibilities, may be subject to such formalities, conditions, restrictions or penalties as are prescribed by law and are necessary in a democratic society, in the interests of national security, territorial integrity or public safety, for the prevention of disorder or crime, for the protection of health or morals, for the protection of the reputation or rights of others, for preventing the disclosure of information received in confidence, or for maintaining the authority and impartiality of the judiciary.

The practical implications of this Article are that consideration must be given as to whether decision-making processes allow for children or adults to adequately express their views and receive information about the decision. We have already seen that these issues may also arise under **Article 6 – the right to a fair hearing** and **Article 8 – the right to respect for family life.**

Article 14: The Right to Enjoy the Convention Rights Without Discrimination

The enjoyment of the rights and freedoms set forth in this Convention shall be secured without discrimination on any ground such as sex, race. colour, language, religion, political or other opinion, national or social origin, association with a national minority, property, birth or other status.

This article does not amount to a general right to equality, rather it imposes a duty to ensure that the rights in the Convention are secured without discrimination. The wording is sufficiently wide to cover sexual orientation, marital status, professional status, being illegitimate and being a prisoner. It would also cover disability, age, being a Traveller or a refugee or asylum-seeker.

It would cover issues such as:

*   Medical treatment being refused on the grounds of age or disability;
*   Effective education not being made available to some groups of children such as Travellers or refugees;
*   Assumptions that children are automatically excluded from participating in decisions about their own medical treatment.

First Protocol Article 2 : The Right to Education

No person shall be denied the right to education. In the exercise of any functions which it assumes in relation to education and to teaching, the State shall respect the right of parents to ensure such education and teaching in conformity with their own religious and philosophical convictions.

The UK placed a reservation on this Article such that the right cannot be enforced if it conflicts with the efficient provision of education to others or involves unreasonable public expenditure.

The following issues may arise under this Article:

- The effects of dispersal on refugee children, if it prevents them from obtaining an effective education;
- The segregation of children with special educational needs or disabilities;
- The adequacy of education for "looked after" children. (See "Learning With Care – The Education of Children Looked After Away From Home" published by The Scottish Executive in March 2001 for an up to date assessment of the need for improvement in this area);
- The adequacy of education for children who are excluded. (It is worth noting that The Education (Scotland) Act 1980 was amended in 2001 to allow a child under 16 to appeal against his or her own exclusion. Prior to this, only parents could appeal on behalf of a child under 16).

Conclusion

Health professionals must recognize that whenever they make decisions they need to bear in mind the human rights dimension. Decision-making needs to be transparent and clients or patients need to have adequate access to sufficient information to allow them to participate effectively in the decision-making process. Clients or patients must have access to a complaints procedure that is as impartial as possible. In view of the possibility of a challenge being made up to one year after an alleged breach of a victim's human rights, the recording of decisions in sufficient detail and with an acknowledgement that human rights were considered, is crucial.

The UN Convention on the Rights of the Child

The UNCRC was ratified by the UK government in 1991. However, unlike the European Convention on Human Rights, it has never been fully incorporated into national law. It is not therefore possible for a child to bring an action against an organization for failure to comply with the UNCRC. Many of the 32 local authorities in Scotland have adopted the UNCRC as a statement of good practice.

The UNCRC is summarised below:
- Every child, regardless of race, colour, sex, language, religion or disability should be protected from every kind of discrimination (Article 2);

- Everyone dealing with children & young people, is obliged to provide the protection & care which puts the child's best interests first (Article 3);
- Every child has the right to life, survival and development (Article 6);
- Every child has the right to a name & nationality from birth (Article 7);
- No child should be separated from their parents against their will unless it is in their best interests (e.g. they are being abused) (Article 9);
- If a child and their parents live in different countries, the child should have the right to keep in touch with each of them on a regular basis. If you or your parents apply to enter or leave any country in order to reunite the family, the application should be dealt with quickly and kindly.(Article 10);
- Every child who is capable of forming an opinion, shall be given the opportunity to express their point of view and have it taken into account, whatever the procedure (Article 12);
- Every child has the right to freedom of expression - that is the right to express their ideas and opinions and obtain information of all kinds (as long as this doesn't endanger the rights of others). (Article 13);.
- Children should have the right to freedom of thought, conscience and religion (Article 14);
- Every child has the right to meet with others - that is to join groups and clubs (unless this violates the rights of others). (Article 15);
- Children should have the right to privacy, and, for example, should not have their letters opened. (Article 16);
- Every child should have access to information which will help their health and well being. (Articles 17);
- Every child should be protected from neglect or abuse (Article 19);
- Children without families including those who are adopted, should be provided with special care and protection & decisions which should be regularly reviewed, should always be based on their best interests (Articles 20, 21 & 25);
- Children who are seeking refugee status, or who have already been deemed to be a refugee under international law should be offered special protection (Article 22);
- Children with disabilities should be offered special help to achieve the greatest possible self reliance so that they can lead a full and active life (Article 23);
- Children should be protected from disease by high quality health care services (Article 24);

- Children and their families should be entitled to social security benefits (Article 26);
- Every country should ensure that parents are able to provide their children with adequate food, clothing and housing (Article 27);
- Children all have the right to an education (Article 28 & 29);
- Children from minority groups should be able to practice their own culture, religion & language. (Article 30);
- Children all have the right to play and enjoy leisure, cultural and artistic pursuits (Article 31);
- Children should be protected from doing work that might damage their health, or from working too long (Article 32);
- Children should be protected from harmful drugs (Article 33);
- Children should be protected from sexual exploitation (Article 34);
- Children should be protected from slavery or any other form of exploitation (Article 35 & 36);
- Children should be protected from torture or other degrading treatment, and if deprived of their liberty should not be kept with adults (Article 37);
- Children should be protected during war (Article 38);
- Children accused of an offence should be informed of the charges against them and offered legal assistance to defend themselves against the charge (Article 40).

Part Eight
Websites & Additional Reading

Part Eight

Websites & Additional Reading

1.   Additional Reading

Social Work Law in Scotland
by Richard Mays, Vikki Smith and Veronica Strachan published by W. Green, Edinburgh. (2nd edition)

Social Work and the Law in Scotland
edited by Deborah, Baillie, Kate Cameron, Lesley-Ann Cull, Jeremy Roche and Janice West published by Palgrave Macmillan, Basingstoke.

Advance Statements About Medical Treatment
published by the British Medical Association, London.

What Should I Do? Guidance on Confidentiality for Nurses, Social Workers, Teachers and Youth Workers
published by Brook Advisory Centres, London

2.   Useful web addresses

The following organisations have useful publications lists and information.

Advocacy Service Aberdeen
www.advocacy.org.uk

Age Concern
www.ageconcern.org.uk

Acts of Parliament
www.hmso.gov.uk/acts

Alzheimer Scotland
www.alzscot.org

Barnardos
www.barnardos.org.uk

British Agencies for Adoption and Fostering
www.baaf.org.uk

British Association of Social Workers
www.basw.org.uk

The British Medical Association
www.bma.org.uk

Capability Scotland
www.capability-scotland.org.uk

Child Policy Network
http://www.childpolicy.org.uk/scotland/index.cfm

Childline
www.childline.org.uk

Children in Scotland
www.childreninscotland.org.uk

Children's Hearings
www.childrens-hearings.co.uk

Children's Rights Information Network
www.crin.org

Commission for Equality and Human Rights
www.equalityhumanrights.com

Commissioner for Children and Young People in Scotland
http://www.sccypr.org

Crown Office and Procurator Fiscal Service
www.crownoffice.gov.uk

DWP
www.dwp.gov.uk

Enable
www.enable.org.uk

Enquire (education/additional support needs)
www.enquire.org.uk

General Medical Council
www.gmc-uk.org.uk

Govan Law Centre Education Law Unit
http://www.edlaw.org.uk

Government Information Service
www.open.gov.uk

Health and Safety Executive
www.hse.gov.uk

Joint Council for the Welfare of Immigrants
www.jcwi.org.uk

The Law Society of Scotland
www.lawscot.org.uk

The Legal Services Agency
www.lsa.org.uk

Mental Welfare Commission
www.mwcscot.org.uk

N.E. Scotland Child Protection Committee
www.nescpc.org.uk

Nursing and Midwifery Council
www.nmc-uk.org

Public Guardian
www.publicguardian-scotland.gov.uk

Royal College of Paediatrics and Child Health
www.rcpch.ac.uk

Save the Children
www.savethechildren.org.uk

Scottish Association of Mental Health
www.samh.org.uk

The Scottish Child Law Centre
www.sclc.org.uk

Scottish Commission for the Regulation of Care
www.carecommission.com

Scottish Consortium for Learning Disability
www.scld.org.uk

The Scottish Courts
www.scotcourts.gov.uk

Scottish Government
www.scotland.gov.uk

Scottish Human Rights Trust
www.scotrights.org

Scottish Information Commissioner
http://www.itspublicknowledge.info

Scottish Legal Aid Board
www.slab.org.uk

Scottish Parliament
www.scottish.parliament.uk

Scottish Public Services Ombudsman
www.spso.org.uk

Scottish Refugee Council
www.scottishrefugeecouncil.org.uk

Shelter in Scotland
www.shelterscotland.org.uk

Who Cares Scotland
www.whocaresscotland.net

Witnesses (resources for)

http://www.scotland.gov.uk/Publications/2005/07/07105526/55283
Being a Witness for Children in Criminal Proceedings

http://www.scotland.gov.uk/Publications/2005/06/28154343/43454
Being a Witness for Young People in Criminal Proceedings

http://www.scotland.gov.uk/Publications/2005/06/2984605/46120
Being a Witness for Children in Children's Hearing Proceedings

http://www.scotland.gov.uk/Publications/2005/06/28141320/13224
Being a Witness for Young People in Children's Hearing Proceedings

http://www.scotland.gov.uk/Publications/2005/06/27110833/08419
Your Child is a Witness – A Booklet for Parents and Carers

http://www.scotland.gov.uk/Publications/2005/06/03104253/42547
Guidance on Special Measures for Vulnerable Child and Adult Witnesses

http://www.scotland.gov.uk/Publications/2007/11/22120443/0
A Guide to the Vulnerable Witnesses (Scotland) Act 2004